Expropriation of U.S. Investments in Cuba, Mexico, and Chile

Eric N. Baklanoff

The Praeger Special Studies program—utilizing the most modern and efficient book production techniques and a selective worldwide distribution network—makes available to the academic, government, and business communities significant, timely research in U.S. and international economic, social, and political development.

Expropriation of U.S. Investments in Cuba, Mexico, and Chile

PRAEGER SPECIAL STUDIES IN INTERNATIONAL ECONOMICS AND DEVELOPMENT

0557093

Praeger Publishers   New York   Washington   London

Library of Congress Cataloging in Publication Data

Baklanoff, Eric N
    Expropriation of U.S. investments in Cuba, Mexico,
and Chile.

    (Praeger special studies in international economics
and development)
    Includes bibliographical references and index.
    1. Investments, American—Chile.   2. Investments,
American—Cuba.   3. Investments, American—Mexico.
I. Title.
HG5160.5.A3B34   332.6'7373   74-6731
ISBN 0-275-09780-3

PRAEGER PUBLISHERS
111 Fourth Avenue, New York, N.Y. 10003, U.S.A.
5, Cromwell Place, London SW7 2JL, England

Published in the United States of America in 1975
by Praeger Publishers, Inc.

Printed in the United States of America

For Lucile and Tanya

This is an impressive and much needed study of a "sore" area relating to economic development in Latin America. In view of the enormous problems that are caused by xenophobic expropriations of U. S. interests and by other comparable measures taken for similar reasons by nationalistic Latin governments—for example, limitations on international transfer of capital—one would think that a comprehensive and inclusive study of this nature would have been undertaken already by many investment organizations, both governmental and private.

But government-sponsored organizations shy away from the idea of identifying a pattern of expropriation, principally because it is their job, in the last analysis, to overcome any expropriatory tendencies. The easiest way to succeed in this is, apparently, to ignore the whole disturbing process.

Perhaps the salient virtue of this book—and it has many virtues—lies in Dr. Eric N. Baklanoff's ability to grasp the close interrelation between political cravings and economic necessities. He sees the connection between underdevelopment and the rise of nationalism, something that he notes particularly well in the chapter on Chile. In turn, he portrays ideological rationalizations such as Marxism in balanced terms that indicate the syndrome of a disease expressed in political as well as economic terms. Yet the author does not suffer from the common, lurking fear that the doom of the entire southern half of the hemisphere to eventual Marxist takeover is inevitable.

In this respect, Dr. Baklanoff draws some inferences that should appear basic to the observer of Latin American political and economic development. In understanding the pattern and casualty of expropriation, it is most important to make a basic <u>political</u> analysis notwithstanding the economic realities of industrial underdevelopment and commercial stagnation. Thus we see here that the nationalistic factor of previous Cuban regimes—the distrust of old Spanish capital—has been an underlying trend in Cuban history that foretold the more virulent and effective antiforeign measures directed at U. S. investment during the Castro regime. We also see that the policies instituted by Fidel Castro and Salvador Allende had much in common with those of the non-Marxist, but extremely nationalistic, regime in Peru as well as with those of the Peron regime in Argentina.

In his chapter on Mexico, Dr. Baklanoff describes how that nation went through the throes of expropriation only to accommodate its nationalistic requirements in other, more symbolic ways. Today, as the author records, Mexico has achieved notable success in "the reconquest of Mexico for the Mexicans" while still attracting foreign capital by developing their own complex, though by no means perfect, formulas. These formulas, again, are not really economic in origin, nor are they ideologically motivated. Rather they are pragmatic political solutions that, though bizarre at times, appear to work in Mexico.

The conclusion is evident: expropriation is often a result of nationalistic factors generated in turn by a need to acquire some form of self-esteem in the absence of adequate national resources. Tragically, the usual effect of uncompensated expropriation is the further impoverishment of a nation's economy and the alienation of possible sources of foreign direct investment, and thus of all external long-term capital—what Dr. Baklanoff calls "The Game Without Winners."

Armistead I. Selden
United States Ambassador to
New Zealand, Tonga, and the Fijis
(Formerly Chairman of the House
Subcommittee on Inter-American
Affairs, 1959-68)

Among the major issues that involve the United States and
Latin American nations in conflict—the Panama Canal question, the
200-mile coastal limit controversy, the diplomatic recognition of
Cuba, the magnitude and terms of economic assistance, the expropriation of U. S. investments—it is the latter that most fundamentally
affects the quality of inter-American relations.

The theme of this volume is the uncompensated or insuffi-
ciently compensated expropriation of U. S. investments in Latin
America. In contrast to nationalization agreements reached through
negotiation, our concern is with unilateral state action by which the
property of a private owner is taken without the provision of "prompt,
adequate, and effective compensation." From the perspective of the
affected foreign investor, expropriation wipes out in a single stroke
assets and future earning prospects of the enterprise.

The focus of this volume is on Mexico, Cuba, and Chile. In
each of these nations a fundamental shift in ideology and internal
power coalitions shaped new policies toward foreign-controlled enterprises that resulted in uncompensated expropriation of U. S. investments on a massive scale. The economic problems of Mexico, Cuba,
and Chile were similar in that they experienced high degrees of external dependency through international trade and the presence of foreign
direct investments in sensitive and strategic industries. They attempted
to eliminate the investment dependency relationship through wholesale
expropriation of foreign-owned properties. Such uncompromising
measures, however, carry no assurance that the venture capital, management, and technology associated with multinational corporations will
be replaced from other sources.

The study's objectives are to (1) set forth and compare the
three significant expropriation experiences—Mexico (1936-38), Cuba
(1959-60), and Chile (1971-73)—in their economic and legal dimen-
sions; (2) analyze the impact of U. S. -controlled enterprises on the
host nations; and (3) evaluate, in the light of these and other expropriation experiences, U. S. investment policy toward Latin America.

In dealing with the perceptions, attitudes, and policies of a
major world region such as Latin America, one must be wary of over-
generalizing. It is nevertheless true that economic nationalism in a
number of Spanish American countries has affected U. S. direct
investment adversely, particularly in the sensitive mineral industries. To capture and illustrate the problems confronting U. S.

investors in the region, one can note two limiting cases. On the one hand, Cuba under Fidel Castro and Chile under the late President Salvador Allende have undergone systemic change under Marxist leadership. On the other hand, since the 1964 April-May revolution, Brazil has pursued a policy of welcoming the inflow of foreign investments to a degree that is exceptional in the hemisphere. The Brazilian generals and tecnicos have adopted consciously a neocapitalistic model of development and look on foreign direct investment as an indispensable instrument in the national quest for development and major power status. These sharply contrasting approaches—the Marxist experiment in Cuba and the "Brazilian Development Model"—may transform Latin America in the 1970s into a scenario of the successes and failures of different political and economic systems.

Private long-term foreign investments customarily are divided into two principal classes—direct investments, in which there is evidence of substantial managerial interest; and portfolio investments, in which the intention of the investor is to realize income or capital gains but not to exercise control over management except as other ordinary stockholders do. Direct investment through multinational enterprises usually brings to the host country, in addition to venture capital, all the elements necessary to create new production units: improved technology, new products and marketing methods, managerial expertise, and entrepreneurial initiative.

The intensification of conflict between some Latin American governments and U.S.-based multinational corporations, ultimately involving the government of the United States, must be viewed in light of five realities. First, U.S. direct investments have become the major channel of U.S.-Latin American economic relations; the value of goods and services produced by Latin American subsidiaries and branches of U.S.-based multinational corporations greatly exceeds U.S. exports to the area. Second, economic nationalism is on the ascendant in a number of the semiindustrialized nations of the region, notably Peru, Mexico, Venezuela, and Argentina. This dynamic force, when joined to either a populist or Marxist political regime, may transform radically the status of foreign investments. From time to time, even right-wing groups, for a variety of motives, support measures prejudicial to foreign investors, including expropriation. Third, as William Glade and others have observed, the bargaining position of many Latin American governments in relation to multinational corporations, is evolving in favor of the former. This change reflects the growing Latin American capabilities in production, finance, and marketing. Fourth, Latin America, which has the fastest demographic growth rate of any major world area, continues to need new risk capital together with advanced managerial and technical resources. The creation of productive jobs for a rapidly urbanizing population presents the region's policymakers with a formidable responsibility. Finally, the U.S. government has encouraged the flow of U.S. direct investment to Latin America through its investment insurance program and other means.

ACKNOWLEDGMENTS

I am grateful to the editors of the following journals and compendia for their permission to publish, in a modified form, portions of articles or chapters that have appeared previously: National Tax Journal, Problemas Internacionales, Intercollegiate Review, Annals of the Southeastern Conference on Latin American Studies, Proceedings of the 58th Annual Conference on Taxation, National Tax Association, Proceedings of the Council on Economics of the American Institute of Mining, Metallurgical and Petroleum Engineers, Inter-American Economic Affairs, and Revolutionary Change in Cuba (Pittsburgh: University of Pittsburgh Press, 1971).

The origin of this book dates back to 1957 when I was doing research on my doctoral dissertation in Chile with the support of a Fulbright scholarship. My study focused on the U. S.-controlled copper mining enterprises and their impact on Chile's economy and balance of international payments. In succeeding years, I continued my study of foreign investments and economic development with the assistance of a postdoctoral fellowship from the Center for Advanced Study in the Behavioral Sciences (1964-65) and a Louisiana State University Research Council grant to participate in the "Workshop on Mexico's Economic Development" at the University of the Americas (summer 1966). A stipend from the University of Alabama Research Grants Committee (summer of 1974) enabled me to revise the manuscript into its final form.

I have also benefited as a participant in the Scholar-Diplomat Seminar sponsored by the U. S. State Department, Bureau of Economic Affairs, during February 1972. My specific project at this week-long seminar concerned U. S. foreign investment policy and the related problem of uncompensated expropriation. Special thanks are due to Robert W. Caldwell, formerly coordinator of the Scholar-Diplomat Seminars, and to W. Robert Warne, financial economist in the Office of Development Finance (ODF), who served as my host officer.

Ambassador Armistead I. Selden has read an earlier version of the manuscript and made valuable observations based on his extended experience as former chairman of the House Subcommittee on Inter-American Affairs. The chapter dealing with U. S. investment policy was strengthened as a result of personal interviews with Sidney Weintraub, deputy assistant secretary, International Finance and Development, U. S. Department of State and Rutherford M. Poats, vice-president for Development, Overseas Private Investment Corporation.

Douglas Lamont, senior academic planner, University of Wisconsin System; Henry Geyelin, executive director of the Council of the Americas; and William Glade, director of the Institute for Latin American Studies, have illuminated for me the role of the multinational corporation in the world of nation-states.

The Cuban chapter has been helped by critiques and suggestions offered by Karl Brandt, professor of economic policy, emeritus, Stanford University; and Carmelo Mesa-Lago, associate professor of economics and associate director of the Center for Latin American studies, University of Pittsburgh.

Thanks are due to Joseph Grunwald, former director of the University of Chile's Economic Institute; Simon Rottenberg, former director of the University of Chicago Cooperative Program in Economics at the Catholic University of Chile; and John Rhodes, former U. S. cultural affairs officer in Santiago, for their assistance in making professional contacts in Chile. The late Herman Max, former director of economic research at the Banco Central de Chile, was generous of his time and gave me access to the bank's reports, monographs, and special studies. Julian Hayes, retired director of public relations, Anaconda Company, Howard L. Edwards, vice president and secretary of Anaconda, and Frank Milliken, president of Kennecott Copper Corporation, have provided me with detailed information regarding their companies' former Chilean subsidiaries. The Chilean chapters have also been strengthened by the suggestions and information given to me by Claudio Bonnefoy, legal advisor in the Chilean Embassy; Richard Goodman, U. S. Treasury Department; Norman Gall and Thomas G. Sanders, both associates with the American Universities field staff; Theodore Moran, Brookings Institution; and Raymond F. Mikesell of the University of Oregon.

My understanding of the "Mexican Development Model" has been enhanced through extended discussion with John Evans and Edward Moseley, both colleagues at the University of Alabama, with Jacqueline Hodgson, University of the Americas, and Richard Greenleaf, director of the Latin American Studies Institute at Tulane University.

Thanks are also due to Mrs. Laura Stapp, Mrs. Cynthia Ruiz-Fornells, Mrs. Linda Barber, and Mrs. Anne Price for their assistance with the revision of chapter drafts.

To my students, both Latin American and North American who have participated in my courses and seminars on Latin American development, I owe a special debt, for they have induced me to clarify my ideas and check my sources.

The analyses and interpretations in this volume, however, are the exclusive responsibility of the author.

CONTENTS

LIST OF TABLES

Table   Page

LIST OF ORGANIZATIONS AND ABBREVIATIONS

AACCLA	Association of American Chambers of Commerce in Latin America
ADELA	Atlantic Community Development Group for Latin America
AID	U. S. Agency for International Development
ASARCO	American Smelting and Refining Company
CECLA	Special Latin American Coordinating Commission
CEMLA	Center for Latin American Monetary Studies
CFE	Federal Electricity Commission (Mexico)
CIPEC	Inter-Governmental Council of Copper Exporting Countries
CNIT	National Chamber of Manufacturing Industries (Mexico)
CODELCO	Chilean Copper Corporation (a government agency)
CORFO	Chilean Development Corporation (a government agency)
CTC	Cuban Labor Confederation
ECLA	United Nations Economic Commission for Latin America
EEC	European Economic Community
FCSC	Foreign Claims Settlement Commission
GNP	Gross National Product
IBRD	International Bank for Reconstruction and Development (World Bank)
ICSID	International Center for the Settlement of Investment Disputes
IDB	Inter-American Development Bank
IMF	International Monetary Fund
ITT	International Telephone and Telegraph Corporation
LAAD	Latin American Agri-business Development Corporation
LAFTA	Latin American Free Trade Association
OAS	Organization of American States
ODEPLAN	Chilean National Planning Office
ODF	Office of Development Finance (U. S. State Department)
OPEC	Organization of Petroleum Exporting Countries
OPIC	Overseas Private Investment Corporation (U. S. government agency)
PEMEX	Petroleos Mexicanos (Mexico's national petroleum agency)
YPF	Yacimentos Petroliferos Fiscales (Argentina's national petroleum agency)

Expropriation of U.S. Investments in Cuba, Mexico, and Chile

U.S. INVESTMENTS
AND THE "RULES OF
THE GAME"

But this much is safe to say: In no area of the world
have the disputes about U. S. investment been so
numerous. Nor in any area of the world—China, Russia,
and Iran under Mossedegh included—has the threat of
nationalization loomed over such a wide array of U. S.
properties, or U. S. business investment been so
important to the broader issues of international relations.
    -William D. Rogers, "United States Investments in
Latin America: A Critical Appraisal, " <u>Virginia
Journal of International Law</u>, 2, no. 2 (March 1971):
247.

The dynamics of economic change in Latin America is the product of two often contradictory forces: the desire for accelerated
development and the quest for national economic independence. These
diverging propensities yield ambivalent policies toward foreign direct
investments. When the balance tilts strongly toward "independence, "
the "rules of the game" may change radically, eventuating in expropriation of foreign-controlled enterprises. More profoundly, Marxist-oriented regimes such as Fidel Castro's Cuba and Salvador
Allende's Chile envision the expropriation of foreign investments as
merely a first step in the radical transformation of the social system.
    This chapter builds a framework for subsequent analysis. It
outlines the scale and pattern of uncompensated expropriations in the
postwar period and addresses itself to several related questions.
How do expropriatory acts become a major problem for U. S. policy
in relation to Latin American states? How do the intellectual and
political climates, particularly the perceived problem of <u>dependencia</u>,

shape and change the "rules of the game" for U. S. investment? Finally, in the absence of an independent judiciary in most Latin American republics, what are the prospects of international arbitration for the settlement of investment disputes?

DEFINITION AND SCALE OF EXPROPRIATIONS

In contrast to nationalization agreements reached through negotiation, our concern is with unilateral state action by which the property of a private owner is taken without the provision of "prompt, adequate and effective compensation. " From the perspective of the affected foreign investor, expropriation wipes out in a single stroke assets and future earnings prospects of the enterprise. [1] In this book the term "expropriation" will be defined as "the procedure by which a state in time of peace and for reasons of public utility appropriates a private property right, with or without compensation, so as to place it at the disposal of its public services, or of the public generally. "[2] Our interest centers on those expropriations, or takings, for which satisfactory compensation was not immediately made, "for they are the ones which have threatened the owners with loss, become issues in international relations, and inhibit foreign investment. "[3] A number of the expropriatory acts discussed here constitute confiscation that may be defined as "any government action by which private property is seized without compensation, no matter in what form or under what name. "[4]

Though uncompensated expropriation continues to be an important and popular form of host government action against foreign enterprises, there have also arisen more elegant and sophisticated forms of foreign wealth deprivation. [5] The term "creeping expropriation" has appeared recently in the literature to describe those indirect measures that may sooner or later produce the same effect as direct confiscation. [6]

The period spanning the expropriation of foreign-owned oil enterprises in Mexico (1938) and the massive confiscation of U. S. properties in Cuba (1959-60) was characterized by the absence of radical change in the "rules of the game. "* Beginning with the Cuban revolution, there have occurred major expropriatory actions involving

---

*There is an exception to this statement. During World War II, properties owned by residents of the Axis powers were nationalized by those Latin American governments that declared war against Germany, Japan, and Italy. The expropriation of tin mines by the Bolivian revolutionary government affected mainly domestic investors.

2

TABLE 1.1

Delayed, Negotiated Settlements on U. S. Properties
in Latin America*
(as of March 1974)

Country		Year of Takeover	Year Settled
Mexico	Plantations and Ranches	1936	1941
	Sinclair Oil Group	1938	1940
	Standard Oil Co. (N. J.)	1938	1942
	Other oil companies	1938	1942
Brazil	American and Foreign Power Co.	1959	1964
	International Tel. and Tel. (ITT)	1962	1967
Argentina	Standard Oil Co. (N. J.)	1963	1967
	10 other oil companies	1963	1967
Bolivia	Gulf Oil Co.	1969	1971
	Mina Matilda Corp. (U. S. Steel and Phillip Brothers)	1971	1972
Peru	W. R. Grace and Co. (sugar plantation)	1969	1974
	W. R. Grace and Co. (industries)	1974	1974
	Cerro de Pasco (agricultural estates)	1969	1974
	Cerro de Pasco (mines and smelters)	1974	1974
	9 other companies	1974	1974

*Note: This table does not include settlements with Chile.

Sources: U. S. State Department, Nationalization, Expropriation, and Other Takings of United States and Certain Foreign Property since 1969, Bureau of Intelligence and Research, (30 November 1971): chs. 3, 6, and Appendix A.

U.S. investments in Brazil (1959 and 1962), Argentina (1963), Peru (1968-74), Bolivia (1969), and Chile (1971-73). A conservative estimate of the value of U.S.-owned assets taken during the 1959-74 period totals about $3.6 billion, as shown below.

(millions of U.S. dollars)

Country	Value of U.S. Claims	Year Settled	Claims Outstanding
Cuba	$1,800	—	$1,800
Brazil	143	1964-67	—
Argentina	200	1967	—
Bolivia	150	1971	—
Peru	500	1974	200
Chile	833	1974	690
TOTAL	$3,626		$2,690

In a number of cases (see Table 1.1) following periods of often difficult and protracted bilateral negotiation, agreements were reached between the expropriating state and the American investor (or U.S. government).

The major outstanding cases of uncompensated expropriation include U.S. properties in Cuba ($1.8 billion); the International Petroleum Corporation in Peru ($200 million); and, in Chile, the U.S. copper mining companies ($537 million) and International Telephone and Telegraph Corporation (ITT—$153 million). In sum, claims of U.S. firms and citizens against Latin American governments as of March 1974 reached a figure of roughly $2.7 billion.

EXPROPRIATION AS A PROBLEM

In a speech delivered in London at a seminar on British-Latin American relations, Galo Plaza, secretary general of the Organization of American States (OAS), suggested that the key to success of private foreign investment is "for both the host country and the foreign investor to agree in advance to abide by mutually acceptable rules of the game. Foremost among these is the soverign right of a country to determine the conditions under which it will accept foreign capital or reject it, either reaping the benefits or bearing the costs of its own decision."[7] The United States' official view is fully in accord with the secretary general's statement. The problem arises when the "rules of the game" are unilaterally and radically altered by the host country, resulting in injury to the foreign investor. Sidney

4

Weintraub, deputy undersecretary of state for international development and finance, expresses the U.S. position in this way, "But once the rules are established and investment has taken place, the host country has the obligation to comply with these rules or to compensate the investors retroactively due to the necessary alteration of these rules."[8]

Uncompensated or inadequately compensated expropriation by foreign states of property owned by U.S. business firms is a major problem for U.S. policy for three basic reasons.[9] First, the United States has a responsibility to protect the property of citizens abroad. Second, such actions can impair good international relations and cause strained relations to deteriorate further. Third, those actions inhibit private investment sought by the United States in less developed countries as a means of promoting their economic development.

Although most of the nations of Latin America adhere to the Calvo Doctrine, the United States contends that a U.S. national abroad may not sign away the right to protection by his government without its consent. Thus, "For its part, the Government of the United States maintains the rules of diplomatic protection, including the rule of exhaustion of local remedies by aliens, as provided by international law."[10] According to the Calvo Doctrine, sovereignty is inviolable, and under no circumstances does the resident alien enjoy the right to have his own government interpose in his behalf. Calvo and his followers "rejected the rather generally accepted principle of international law which requires states to maintain a minimum standard of treatment of foreigners no matter how they treat their own nationals."[11]

The United States has acknowledged consistently the right of a sovereign nation to expropriate foreign-owned property, as long as the taking conformed to the standards of international law, that is, that it was for a public purpose, not discriminatory against U.S. citizens, and accompanied by just compensation.[12] Even when just compensation is made, expropriation is viewed by the United States government as a policy that in most cases, is not in the interest of the low-income nation. The reasons given for this position are that (1) payment of the required compensation diverts resources needed for economic development and depletes supplies of foreign exchange (2) property is often transferred from competent private hands to governments that lack the requisite managerial skills; and (3) such actions tend to worsen the climate for private investment.

U.S. INVESTMENTS AND ECONOMIC NATIONALISM

To extract the constructive mobilizing effect of nationalism in Latin America without falling prey to its

intoxicating and irrational aspects is in fact one of the
major tasks not only of economists but also of political
scientists, politicians, and statesmen.
　—Roberto de Oliveira Campos, Reflections on Latin
American Development (Austin: University of Texas
Press, 1967), p. 5.

　　　Antipathy toward external (particularly U. S.) direct investments in Latin America is shared by numerous and diverse interest
groups. The cultural elite are wary of the foreign business presence
because of its impact on Hispanic culture. Local enterprises may
resent foreign-controlled firms because of "disloyal" competition.
The "progressive" group of Roman Catholic bishops and priests in
Latin America ascribe much of the blame for the region's economic
backwardness to international capitalism, particularly foreign investment. Still others believe that multinational corporations decapitalize
the host nation through the balance of international payments. A more
recent criticism of multinational enterprise in Latin America
derives from the new "dependence theorists. "
　　　The belief that foreign direct investments are wealth diminishing rather than wealth enhancing is by no means confined to Marxist-
oriented intellectuals. [13] Among moderate (in contrast to radical)
thinkers in Latin America there exists an important body of opinion
that accepts the balance of payments drain thesis. This point is well
illustrated by the meeting of the Special Latin American Coordinating
Commission (CECLA), attended in May 1969 by ministerial level
delegations from all Organization of American States (OAS) nations
except the United States. The CECLA conference produced agreements on key development issues, including the role of foreign direct
investments. The "Latin American Consensus of Vina del Mar, " the
main document produced by the meeting, was presented to President
Richard M. Nixon the following month at an official ceremony at the
White House witnessed by Latin American ambassadors. In remarks
after the presentation ceremony, Gabriel Valdes, president of the
special commission, stated that private foreign investments "have
meant, and mean today for Latin America that the amounts that leave
our Continent are many times higher than those that are invested in
it. Our potential capital is diminishing while the profits of the
invested capital grow and multiply at enormous rate, not in our countries, but abroad. "[14]
　　　Mr. Valdes' assertion contrasts sharply with the findings of
the joint report of the OAS and the Economic Commission for Latin
America (ECLA), whose careful analysis is based on empirical studies conducted in the larger Latin American nations. The OAS-ECLA
report concludes that profit remittances in a dynamic economy tend

6

to constitute only a small portion of the additional foreign exchange proceeds (or exchange savings) generated by the investment. [15] Empirically supported cost-benefit analyses such as those made available by the Council of the Americas and the OAS will not change the receptivity of these groups to foreign private investment.

Osvaldo Sunkel, one of the new "dependence theorists," believes that the recent burst of nationalism in Latin America "is in fact a reaction to a long-term and increasingly intolerable dependence on foreigners." [16] The Brazilian political scientist, Helio Jaguaribe, defines "national development" as "that kind of growth which leads to maximizing the control of the nation over its own means and resources." [17] "Autonomy," for him, "is the crucial question of socio-economic development and is both a condition for its promotion and an objective for its achievement." [18] Miguel S. Wionczek, an economist associated with the Mexican-based Center for Latin American Monetary Studies (CEMLA), argues that multinational corporations wish to perpetuate the political and economic dependence of Latin America on industrial countries, particularly the United States. And he predicted that these efforts to maintain the region in a dependency relationship "represent probably the single most important element in the growing conflict between foreign private capital and Latin American societies." [19]

Simon G. Hanson, a seasoned observer of U. S.-Latin American economic relations, points to the absence of a common purpose joining the American republics in the Alliance for Progress. Specifically, in the case of direct investment, the United States was proceeding on the premise that Latin America was prepared to mobilize its resources fully to accelerate economic development. Latin America, however, "was proceeding on the theory that its primary interest is a political aim—to reestablish local control of its resources even though this might slow economic development. And Latin America assumed the United States understood this." [20]

The "Brazilian Model" contrasts sharply with the approaches to development taken by several Spanish American countries. Since the 1964 revolution, Brazil's generals and tecnicos have consciously forged a neocapitalistic economic system in which foreign direct investment plays a critical role.

From 1967-72 the flow of new investments by multinational companies in Brazil reached nearly $1.8 billion[21] and contributed to the phenomenal acceleration of the nation's economic growth. Foreign direct investments, many in joint ventures with Brazilian partners, have favored Brazil's petrochemical, steel, shipbuilding, pulp and paper, iron-ore, aluminum, and automotive industries. Government strategy regarding foreign investment, according to former minister of planning, Joao Paulo dos Reis Velloso, aims at the

7

establishment of large companies with the majority of shares held by private investors, both foreign and domestic, in areas requiring advanced technology and management.

One of the concomitants of the new nationalism in Latin America is the objective of a reduced dependency on the United States. Many Latin American countries, both at the national level and within hemispheric organizations such as the OAS and the Inter-American Development Bank (IDB), are moving with increasing speed to diversify their international relations with the rest of the world. The recent granting of permanent observer status in the Organization of American States to Canada, Guiana, Israel, Italy, the Netherlands, Spain, and France is significant in this context. Trade expansion with Western Europe, Japan, and Canada, together with new direct investments from these sources, are viewed as desirable steps to reduce what many Latin Americans regard as an intrusive U. S. presence in the area.

INTERNATIONAL ARBITRATION: A VIABLE ALTERNATIVE?

The absence of an independent judiciary in most Latin American republics suggests that the courts cannot be expected to provide an objectively fair settlement on litigation involving a U. S. affiliate and a Latin American government. In these nations, with the possible exceptions of Brazil, Venezuela, and Chile, there is very little respect for the integrity of supreme courts and no real tradition of judicial independence. "Legal guarantees," according to Arpad von Lazar, "are not often observed, judicial tenure is not respected, and courts are suspended or excessively limited in their jurisdiction."[22] In July 1971 President Salvador Allende signed into law a constitutional amendment specifically denying the large U. S.-owned copper companies the right of recourse through the regular courts of law to the Chilean Supreme Court.

If neither domestic adjudication nor bilateral negotiations provide a solution, what are the prospects of moving an unresolved dispute between a U. S. investor and a Latin American state to a setting where international conciliation and arbitration can proceed? An important development in the sphere of international arbitration has been the establishment of the International Center for the Settlement of Investment Disputes (ICSID), under the auspices of the International Bank for Reconstruction and Development. Since the convention establishing the center entered into force in October 1966, a growing number of international investment agreements have incorporated provisions for recourse to its facilities.

As is typically the case in arbitration matters, recourse to the center is entirely voluntary. Ratification of the Convention on the Settlement of Investment Disputes between States and Nationals of Other States does not bind a country to submit any particular dispute to the center. However, once a state and a foreign investor have agreed to submit their cases, they must comply with the arbitral award. Although it is recognized that the laws of most countries make it impossible to enforce a judgment against a sovereign state, the official feeling is that few governments are likely to violate their treaty obligations under the convention by refusing to honor an arbitration award.

Since the convention came into force, 68 states have signed and 65 have ratified it. [23] Significantly, no Latin American governments have signed the convention. An early effort was made by A. Broches, secretary-general of the center, to persuade the Latin American nations to sign the convention. In an address delivered on 27 May 1965 in San Juan Puerto Rico, to a joint meeting of the Section of International and Comparative Law of the American Bar Association, he presented his refutation of the five principal arguments that had been advanced in Latin America against the convention. As far as is known, no response has ever appeared in the Latin American jurisprudential literature. [24] Actual and potential foreign investors have tried to persuade competent Latin American authorities to join the center, and some multinational corporations apparently have indicated that they consider the possibility of relying on the convention a significant factor in reaching an investment decision. [25]

A major Latin American objection derives directly from the Calvo Doctrine: "Any form of intervention, even if only diplomatic, by a government in favor of one of its investors operating abroad, is an impermissible interference in the internal affairs of the State. "[26] In analyzing this objection, Paul C. Szasz clearly shows that under article 27 (1) of the convention, consent to arbitrate relieves the host government of any diplomatic importunities by the investor's state. The investor's state is enjoined from giving diplomatic protection unless the host government "shall have failed to abide by and comply with the award rendered in such a dispute. "[27]

Among the important deliberations of the Special Latin American Coordinating Commission (CECLA) during its ninth extraordinary meeting held January 1971 in Brasilia was a draft project submitted by the World Bank providing for the creation of an International Insurance Agency. The proposal, designed to provide insurance coverage for the political risk of expropriation, was rejected unanimously by the CECLA delegates. [28] The main objection to such an agency was that the proposal provided for an international arbitration board, which it was felt likely would infringe on the sovereignty of the participating states.

The foregoing discussion indicates that there is little prospect of moving an unresolved dispute between a U. S. investor and a Latin American government to a setting where international conciliation and arbitration can proceed.

NOTES

1. Franklin Root, "The Expropriation Experience of American Companies," Business Horizons 11, no. 2 (April 1968): 69

2. S. Friedman, Expropriation in International Law (London: Stevens and Sons, 1953), p. 3.

3. U. S., Congress, House, Committee on Foreign Affairs, Expropriation of American-owned Property by Foreign Governments in the Twentieth Century, 88th Cong., 1st Sess., 1963, p. 3 (hereinafter referred to as Committee on Foreign Affairs, Expropriation of American-owned Property).

4. P. Adriaanse, Confiscation in Private International Law (The Hague: Martinus Nikjhoff, 1956), p. 8.

5. J. Frederick Truitt, "Expropriation of Foreign Investment: Summary of the Post World War II Experience of American and British Investors in the Less Developed Countries," Journal of International Business Studies (Fall 1970): 21-34.

6. Simon G. Hanson, Dollar Diplomacy Modern Style (Washington, D. C.: Inter-American Press, 1970), p. 65.

7. Alliance for Progress Weekly Newsletter 10, no. 22 (29 May 1972).

8. Sidney Weintraub, "La Politica de Estados Unidos sobre Inversiones de Capital Privado en Desarrollo," El Mercado de Valores 32, no. 52 (25 December 1972): 1426.

9. Committee on Foreign Affairs, Expropriation of American-owned Property, op. cit., p. vii.

10. Ninth International Conference of American States, Report of the Delegation of the United States of America (Washington, D. C.: Government Printing Office, 1948), p. 200.

11. J. Lloyd Mecham, A Survey of United States Latin American Relations (Boston: Houghton Mifflin, 1965), p. 95.

12. Committee on Foreign Affairs, Expropriation of American-owned Property, op. cit., pp. 22-23.

13. The Marxist-oriented social commentators Paul Baran and Paul Sweezy argue that foreign investment, "far from being a means of developing under-developed countries, is a most efficient device for transferring wealth from poorer to richer countries." Paul

Baran and Paul M. Sweezy, "Notes on the Theory of Imperialism," in Problems of Economic Dynamics and Planning: Essays in Honor of Michael Kalecki (Warsaw: Polish Scientific Publishers, 1964), p. 161.

14. Alliance for Progress Weekly Newsletter 7, no. 5 (23 June 1969).

15. U. N., Department of Economic and Social Affairs, Foreign Private Investment in the Latin American Free-Trade Area (New York: United Nations, 1961), pp. 13-14.

16. Osvaldo Sunkel, "Business and Dependencia, A Latin American View," Foreign Affairs 50, no. 3 (April 1972): 517.

17. Raymond Vernon, ed., How Latin America Views the U. S. Investor (New York: Praeger Publishers, 1966), p. 68.

18. Ibid., p. 85.

19. Vernon, op. cit., p. 50.

20. Hanson, op. cit., p. 43.

21. Embassy of Brazil, Brazil Today, no. 21 (28 September 1973).

22. Arpad von Lazar, Latin American Politics: A Primer (Boston: Allyn and Bacon, 1971), p. 41; on this point see also Martin C. Needler, Latin American Politics in Perspective (Princeton, N. J.: C. Van Nostrand, 1967), pp. 153-55.

23. International Center for the Settlement of Investment Disputes, Seventh Annual Report 1972/1973, Washington, D. C. Membership includes the United States, 31 African, 18 European, 12 Asian, and 6 other nations.

24. See Paul C. Szasz, "The Investment Disputes Convention in Latin America," Virginia Journal of International Law 2, no. 2 (March 1971): 258.

25. Ibid., p. 259.

26. Ibid., p. 260.

27. Ibid., footnote 18.

28. El Mercado de Valores 31, no. 1 (15 March 1971): 169.

2

U.S. INVESTMENTS AND THE ORIGINS OF THE CUBAN REVOLUTION: A REJOINDER

A major thesis advanced to explain Cuba's transformation into a Marxist-Leninist state centers on that nation's presumed economic and social backwardness prior to 1959.[1] The "backwardness" thesis is often supported by a corollary: the alleged exploitative grip by which U. S. investors held the Cuban economy. Marvin D. Bernstein, for example, seems to accept this corollary.

> If private capital ever had the chance, through its economic and political influence, to demonstrate its ability to improve the lot of a people while still earning profits, American private capital did in Cuba. Castro is a chicken come home to roost.[2]

American investments, in the view of a number of U. S. and Latin American writers, were responsible for distorting and inhibiting the development of the Cuban economy prior to the revolution. For example, Edward Boorstein contends that the U. S. companies interrupted the normal process of capitalist development in Cuba, turned the island into a sugar plantation, prevented native industrialization, and transformed the country into a mere appendage of the U. S. economy.[3] Maurice Zeitlein and Robert Scheer claim that U. S. direct investments "contributed heavily to Cuba's overspecialization, economic instability, and stagnation."[4] They further allege that the U. S. firms from their secure economic and political positions in Cuba could have initiated new ventures but failed to do so. James O'Connor, in his recent work, The Origin of Socialism in Cuba,[5] states his belief that the investment policies of the foreign-owned corporations were at odds with Cuba's needs. The way out of this impasse, according to most of these critics, was for Cuba to achieve full independence from the United States through a socialist revolution.

The aim of this chapter is to evaluate the foregoing criticisms in the light of economic analysis and the available data. Our investigation of the role of U. S. direct investments in Cuba's development spans roughly four decades, from the early 1920s to the moment of expropriation in 1959-60. Particular attention is given to the postwar years 1946-59.

I have used information compiled by the U. S. Department of Commerce, United Nations agencies, and Cuba's central bank, Banco Nacional de Cuba. The encyclopedic work of the Cuban Economic Research Project, Un Estudio Sobre Cuba (1963), the World Bank's Report on Cuba (1951), H. C. Wallich's Monetary Problems of an Export Economy: the Cuban Experience, 1914-1947 (1950), and Boris Goldenberg's The Cuban Revolution and Latin America (1965) have also been of valuable assistance.

ANATOMY OF AN EXPORT ECONOMY

In organization and structure, Cuba until the early 1950's typified what economists have come to call an "export economy."[6] Such an economy exhibits the following properties: a high ratio of export production to total output in the cash sector of the economy; a concentrated export structure; substantial inflow of long-term capital, including the presence of foreign-owned enterprises; and a high marginal propensity to import. Commonly in such an economy, government revenues are tied closely to the oscillations of export income. The export sector constitutes the dynamic, autonomous variable that powers the nation's development; it is also the short-run disturber. The sheer weight of exports in relation to total economic activity dictates that the external market rather than private investment or government expenditure exercise predominant influence on aggregate demand. Because of its specialized structure, the export economy is heavily dependent on foreign sources for many kinds of consumer and capital goods.

As Henry C. Wallich observed, the "main and very great advantage that underdeveloped export economies enjoy is precisely that they do not have to create a modern economy entirely out of their own resources—a process that took Europe centuries to accomplish."[7] His point applies with particular force to Cuba with its relatively small population and specialized tropical resources.

Cuba's sugar "sector," including cane growing and the industrial and commercial income from the milling and marketing of raw sugar, contributed directly between one-fourth and one-third of the national income in the 1946-59 period. Sugar brought in between 80 percent and 90 percent of Cuba's external receipts from exports and thereby constituted the "great independent variable," the "master beam," of the island's economy. By emphasizing specialization and extreme interdependence with the world (mainly the U. S.) economy, Cuba was able to achieve what was probably the highest standard of living among tropical nations. *

On the negative side, because of the central position of sugar in Cuba's exports and national product, the nation suffered from chronic seasonal unemployment. Economic activity oscillated between the zafra, the grinding period, and the dead season, June through December, when unemployment normally reached a level of 20 percent and much capital equipment remained idle. Before the postwar diversification drive, Cuba's relatively "open" economy resulted in her vulnerability to "imported" booms and recessions that defied the possibility of effective compensatory measures by government. The unemployment problem for sugar workers in the latter 1950s was mitigated to some degree by the availability of alternative job opportunities. During 1958, for example, one-fourth of the cane labor worked for two or three months in the coffee harvest, which preceeded the zafra; other off-season jobs were available in rice farming, construction, and in the maintenance of sugar mills. However, the "vast majority of seasonally employed workers returned to the family farms, grew subsistence crops on plots furnished by the sugar mills, or eked out a bare subsistence on credits furnished by local stores."[8]

On the eve of the Cuban Revolution, in 1958, the United States was purchasing two-thirds of the island's exports and was supplying 70 percent of its imports. Next to Brazil, Cuba was the most important Latin American source of agricultural imports for the United States. During the five-year period 1954-58, the United States purchased three-fourths of Cuba's tobacco and 60 percent of its sugar. Raw Cuban sugar was sold to the United States under a quota system at prices that in most years were substantially above the world price.[9] Both the quota and the more stable U. S. premium price helped to curb the annual fluctuations of Cuban sugar sales abroad.

---

*Paul Hoffman, former administrator of the Marshall Plan, classified 100 underdeveloped countries of the world into four categories by average per capita income. Fifty-two fell in the under $100 a year category, 23 in the $100-199 category, 16 in the $200-299 category, and 9 in the $300-699 category. Cuba is one of the top nine. P. G. Hoffman, One Hundred Countries, One and One Quarter Billion People, (Washington, D. C.: Committee for International Economic Growth, 1960).

Cuba's relatively small domestic market, its location on the threshold of the United States, the largest "common market" in the world with which it had concluded preferential trade agreements, its tropical climate, and specialized resource endowment—these and other factors conditioned the island's intimate commercial and financial ties with the United States.

U.S. INVESTMENTS IN HISTORICAL PERSPECTIVE

U. S. direct investments in Cuba increased sharply after the Spanish American War of 1898 and the establishment of a special political relationship between the island and the United States (codified in the Platt Amendment). The amendment, which was incorporated in a permanent treaty and signed at Havana on 22 May 1903, provided, among other things, "that the United States may exercise the right to intervene for the preservation of Cuban independence, the maintenance of a government adequate for the protection of life, property, and individual liberty. . . . "[10] The Platt Amendment was formally abrogated by President Franklin Roosevelt on 29 May 1934. Lloyd Mecham, an authority on U. S. -Latin American relations wrote, "That it would have been handy, many years later, to have the Platt Amendment in reserve when Fidel Castro imposed Communism on Cuba, can hardly be denied. "[11] U. S. investments in the island rose from $44 million in 1897 to $253 million in 1914. [12] During the First World War the value of U. S. business holdings in Cuba doubled, and investments continued their advance during the 1920s, reaching $919 million at the end of 1929—the highest of the interwar period.

The flow of U. S. investments to Cuba in the 1920s was associated closely with the violent sugar crisis of 1920-21. With the end of wartime sugar controls in the United States, the price of sugar rose from 5. 9 cents a pound in 1918 to an all-time peak of 22. 5 cents in 1920, followed, after the recovery of European sugar beet production, by a spectacular drop to 1. 8 cents in 1921. "This economic extravaganza, " in the words of the U. S. Department of Commerce, "was quickly followed by a catastrophic crash in the autumn of 1920, which wrested control of the most sensitive areas of Cuban economic life, sugar and banking, from domestic hands and brought United States interests, particularly banking, into unsought preeminence. "[13] Many Cuban-owned sugar centrals and banks went into bankruptcy and were purchased by U. S. interests. Thus, numerous family enterprises, whose financial and managerial resources proved inadequate in the crisis, were absorbed by U. S. corporate capital.

The economist naturally witnesses these events with mixed feelings. On the one hand, the passing of key economic activities into

TABLE 2.1

U.S. Direct Investments in Cuba, by Sector,
for 1929, 1946, and 1959
(millions of U.S. dollars)

Industry	1929	Percent	1946	Percent	1959	Percent	Value Increment 1946–59
Agriculture	575	62.6	227	41.0	a	—	a
Public Utilities	215	23.4	253	45.8	313	32.7	60
Manufacturing	45	4.9	40	7.2	115	12.0	75
Commerce	a	—	12	2.2	44	4.6	32
Petroleum b	9	1.0	14	2.5	143	15.0	129
Other	75	8.2	8	1.4	341	35.7	
Total	919	100.0	553	100.0	956	100.0	403

aIncluded in "other."

bRefineries and marketing only.

Sources: U. S. Department of Commerce, Investment in Cuba (Washington, D. C.: Government Printing Office, 1956), p. 10, table 5; U. S. Investments in the Latin American Economy (Washington, D. C.: Government Printing Office, 1957), p. 175, table 95; and Survey of Current Business 40, no. 9 (September 1960): 20, table 1.

foreign ownership constituted a psychic blow to Cuba's national posture, coming so soon after the winning of the island's independence from Spain. On the other, the reorganization and modernization of Cuba's sugar industry under U. S. private initiative at this critical time gave the island a competitive edge and assured Cuba of its future leadership in the world sugar economy. The island could overcome lower sugar prices by more efficient production and a greatly expanded volume: average annual production of sugar in Cuba increased from 2. 3 million short tons (12. 5 percent of world production) in 1911-15 to 5. 3 million tons in 1926-30 (18 percent of world production). [14] Sugar and its products again could be counted on to provide the "engine of economic growth. " By the mid-1920s, U. S. -owned sugar mills were producing almost two-thirds of the Cuban sugar crop. [15]

Cuba ranked first in Latin America in the value of U. S. direct investments in 1929. As Table 2. 1 shows, these holdings were strongly concentrated in sugar production ($575 million) and public services (over $200 million); together, they accounted for 86 percent of the total. By the end of the 1920s, U. S. capital had created an islandwide electric power system and organized and financed a substantial fraction of Cuba's railways.

Cuba, like other Latin American countries whose economies were export-oriented, was jolted by the Great Depression. The nation's sugar industry was especially vulnerable to a contraction of world demand; and after 1929 the value of Cuban exports fell sharply, reflecting mainly the weakness of sugar prices. United States business holdings in Cuba, which had accumulated so swiftly during World War I and the 1920s (through the reinvestment of earnings in sugar enterprises[16] and the establishment of new firms), contracted for almost a decade and a half. The value of U. S. direct investments reached its nadir in 1943 ($529 million)—a very substantial decline, reflecting the "revaluation of assets and reorganization of overextended corporate activities. "[17] As one would expect, the heaviest losses were sustained by the sugar companies, whose investments were cut by more than half their 1929 value.

CUBA'S RESOURCE ENDOWMENT AND STANDARD OF LIVING

The living standard of a nation rests on the skills and energies of its people, the quantity and quality of its natural resources, and the amount and composition of the economy's accumulated capital stock. Cuba in the latter 1950s already had evolved important professional, technical, and managerial middle groups and a substantial pool of skilled workers. Many of the country's energetic and competent

17

administrators were "schooled in large-scale operations through the great development of the sugar industry and other enterprises."[18] Spanish immigrants, particularly those who came to Cuba during the first quarter of the twentieth century, contributed disproportionately to the island's stock of high level manpower resources.

About 80 percent of the Cuban land mass was under cultivation or used for grazing in the 1950s. The topsoil is exceedingly fertile, deep, rich, and well watered, and the topography is favorable to widespread use of farm machinery. An absence of climatic variation, however, limits the island to the cultivation of tropical and semitropical crops and to livestock raising. Domestic production supplied about 70 percent of Cuba's food consumption. The island also contains important iron ore and nickel mineral reserves and useful deposits of manganese, chrome, copper, and limestone. And it is favored with several large, well-protected natural harbors. The energy resources constitute the island's major deficiency, for Cuba has no coal, and very little oil has been discovered thus far.

Cuba was one of the most capitalized nations in Latin America. In 1951 the World Bank Mission observed that

> In the 161 sugar centrales, in the excellent central
> highway, in the extensive system of public and private
> railroads, in the harbor installations, in the cities
> and their utilities, Cuba has the basis of exceptionally
> fine equipment for modern economic activity and further
> development.[19]

An extensive, well-integrated system of highways provided the basis for the rapid postwar advance in the island's motorized transport industry. In mid-1957, prior to the intensification of guerrilla warfare, Cuba's central bank possessed $535 million in gold and foreign exchange reserves. Among her sister republics, only Venezuela had accumulated larger foreign reserves.

Cuba, in sharp contrast to Bolivia, Ecuador, Mexico, and Peru, had a very small rural subsistence sector. The island could not match the prosperity of the industrially advanced nations of the North Atlantic: the United States, Canada, and the Northwest European countries. However, compared with other nations in Latin America, Cuba in the 1950s possessed one of the most advanced economies and ranked high in the general level of living afforded its citizens. According to the World Bank Mission

> The general impression of members of the Mission,
> from observations in travels all over Cuba, is that
> living levels of the farmers, agricultural laborers,

industrial workers, storekeepers, and others, are higher all along the line than for corresponding groups in other tropical countries and in nearly all other Latin American countries. This does not mean that there is no dire poverty in Cuba, but simply that in comparative terms Cubans are better off, on the average, than the people of these other areas. [20]

As is true of the other Latin American countries, there existed in Cuba a substantial disparity in the level of social development (that is, literacy, health care, housing) between the prosperous capital province and some of the more backward rural provinces.

In 1957 Cuba's real income per capita (national income divided by the population) was $378 or fourth in Latin America. [21] Only Venezuela, Argentina, and Uruguay ranked above Cuba. Moreover, the other two nations in the Hispanic cultural world, Spain ($324) and Portugal ($212), failed to reach the Cuban level. Except for Venezuela, Cuba probably enjoyed the highest per capita income among all countries in the wet tropical zone, extending from the Tropic of Cancer to the Tropic of Capricorn. Other measures provide a better approximation of the degree to which real income was shared among the population. For example (in 1957 or 1958), Cuba ranked third in Latin America as reflected in the following indices:[22] per capita daily calorie consumption, per capita meat consumption, per capita steel consumption, per capita paper consumption, radios per 1,000 persons, and the ratio of physicians to population. The island had achieved the lowest mortality rate (6.5 per 1,000 inhabitants) and lowest infant mortality rate (38 per 1,000 inhabitants) in Latin America. In 1959 Cuba had one million radios and the highest ratio of television sets per 1,000 inhabitants.

Benjamin Higgins, whose work in economic development generally is regarded highly for its theoretical rigor and thorough documentation, appears partially to have accepted the "backwardness thesis." In a chapter entitled "Cuba: The Anatomy of a Revolution," he writes that Cuba's relatively high per capita income "does not properly indicate the extent of poverty, ignorance, and ill health that prevailed in Cuba in 1958."[23] But as we have shown, the opposite is the case. The several socioeconomic indices cited above, particularly those relating to health, indicate that within the Latin American context the per capita income understated the general level of living afforded Cuba's people. Higgins' statement that Cuba's illiteracy "was about equal to the Latin American average, about 40 percent" is contradicted by U.N. statistics that show that 79 percent of the population 15 years and above was literate in 1958.

With an organized labor force of over 1.5 million workers, Cuba ranked with Uruguay and Argentina in the degree of unionization. The island's unionized workers enjoyed the protection of what was probably the most comprehensive labor code in Latin America. Ernest Schwarz, the executive secretary of the CIO's Committee on Latin American Affairs, gave his impressions of the achievements of Cuba's labor federation (CTC) as follows:

> The CTC has enabled the Cuban workers to set an example to others of what can be achieved by labor unity and strength. Wages are far above those paid in many other parts of the Caribbean or, for that matter, Latin America. In addition, the eight-hour working day forms the basis for every one of the collective contracts concluded by the CTC's affiliated organizations. Modern types of social protection and insurance are provided in laws, public statutes, or union contracts; while funds maintained and administered in common by labor, employers, and the authorities provide adequate means to put them into practice. The sugar workers union alone, to cite one example, disposes of such a fund in the amount of half a billion dollars, and its insurance covers medical attention, sickness, and accidents during and out of work. The CTC, moreover, has taken up a place of full responsibility within the Cuban community as a whole, and at present develops its own economic program to compensate for the seasonal nature of employment and production in the sugar industry. Today, the Confederation counts more than a million members—with its 500,000 sugar workers constituting the most powerful of the thirty-five national federations affiliated with it and representing every branch of industry and agriculture on the island. The Confederation has drawn every fifth Cuban into its ranks, and has thus obtained a much higher numerical degree of organization in proportion to population than, for example, the much larger movement in the United States. [24]

The level of wages in Cuban manufacturing contributed significantly to the nation's relatively high living standards. In 1957 wages averaged $6 for an eight-hour day in manufacturing as a whole and ranged from over $4 for unskilled workers to $11 for skilled employees in Cuba's sugar mills. [25] Real wages in Cuba were higher than any country in the Western Hemisphere, excepting the United States and Canada.

THE PATTERN OF U.S. INVESTMENT FLOW, 1946-59

Following the Second World War, Cuba's investment climate was one of the most favorable in Latin America. Constitutional guarantees continued in force in the protection of property rights, and these applied equally to foreigners and to Cubans. [26] The nation enjoyed financial stability throughout the period analyzed. In sharp contrast to the more general postwar experience in Latin America, Cuba's cost of living remained stable, the peso continued at par with the U.S. dollar, and foreign exchange operations were free of control. Until the installment of the Castro regime, profits, interest, and other factor payments could be remitted freely abroad; and the risk of currency devaluation was negligible.

From 1946 on, new U.S. investments in Cuba (see Table 2.1) assumed a highly diversified pattern and flowed into a broad spectrum of Cuba's economic activities: infrastructure, manufacturing and commerce, petroleum refining, diversified agriculture, mining, and the tourist industry. The augmented production capabilities represented by U.S. subsidiaries and branches in Cuba, primarily directed to meet the requirements of the local market, both stimulated and responded to the postwar expansion of Cuba's economy. They were decisive in the growth of electric power and telephone service, in the rapid advance of petroleum refining and nickel mining, and paced the diversification and growth of manufacturing.

Of the $403 million increment in U.S. business holdings in Cuba from 1946-59, petroleum refining accounts for $129 million, manufacturing for $75 million, public services for $60 million, and commerce for $32 million. New investments in diversified agriculture, mining, and hotels explain the remaining $107 million. Nearly a fifth of the postwar increment in U.S. business investments ($75 million), it is interesting to observe, was added in 1959—during Premier Fidel Castro's first year in power. This sizeable investment flow to Cuba "represented the continuation of large expansion programs of mining and utility companies, and the extension of credit to subsidiaries of petroleum companies during that year. "[27]

The Cuban Telephone Company, a subsidiary of ITT Corporation, increased its capital investment from $32 million in 1945 to $70 million in 1955. [28] After reaching an agreement on rates with the Cuban government, the company embarked in 1957 on a major expansion plan involving a programmed investment of $85 million. [29] The Cuban Electric Company, a subsidiary of American and Foreign Power Corporation, followed a similar pattern. Its facilities were increased during 1948-53 in response to the growing demand for electricity and, shortly thereafter, the company set out on another expansion program for the period 1956-61.

U. S. investments in petroleum refining advanced sharply from $14 million in 1946 to $143 million in 1959, stimulated by the tax exemption legislation of the Industrial Promotion Law. Cuba achieved self-sufficiency in petroleum refining at the end of 1959 with a capacity of 83,000 barrels per day supplied exclusive by two U. S. subsidiaries and the Royal Dutch-Shell group.[30]

	Capacity (barrels per day)
Texaco	20,000
Esso	35,000
Royal Dutch-Shell	28,000

American investments in manufacturing nearly tripled from 1946-59 (from $40-115 million), thereby pacing Cuba's postwar growth in this sector. They were particularly prominent in chemicals and allied products ($28 million) and food products ($21 million).[31] In the 1950s, Procter and Gamble Corporation of Cuba, S. A., established the first detergent plant in that nation, which was also the first in Latin America. Finally, U. S. investments in Cuban commercial establishments rose appreciably during the period analyzed and supported the island's well-developed commercial sector.

According to the Cuban Economic Research Group at the University of Miami, the progress made by the mining industry in Cuba during the 1940-58 period was due, in great part, to the geological studies carried out between 1940 and 1945 by the U. S. Geological Survey. With the operation of the U. S. government-built Nicaro Nickel Company (valued at $110 million) and the Moa Bay Mining Company, a subsidiary of Freeport Sulphur Company (representing a total outlay of $119 million, including a $25 million housing project for company employees), "Cuba assured itself a position as a major supplier of nickel in the world."[32]

THE DIVERSIFICATION DRIVE, 1952-58

The diversification of Cuba's industrial park and a growing capacity to meet food requirements out of domestic production substantially lessened the island's dependence on world sugar markets in the postwar period. Not only did Cuban exports decline as a share of national income, but sugar also played a diminishing role in commodity exports between the latter 1940s and latter 1950s.

Sugar and its by-products constituted 89 percent of the value of Cuba's commodity exports during 1947-49, compared with 80 percent during 1954-58; and the ratio of total exports to national income declined from 41 percent to 33 percent for the same periods, respectively. Despite the stagnation in the value of sugar exports from the latter 1940s to the latter 1950s, the Cuban economy experienced a powerful upward trend in fixed capital formation, both private and public, signifying growing autonomy of this key variable from the exigencies of international trade.

Diversification of Cuba's balance of payments position was materially strengthened in the 1950s by the development of the island's tourist industry and the growth of export earnings for products other than sugar. The expanded operations of the U. S. government-constructed Nicaro Nickel Company and the Moa Bay Mining Company, a subsidiary of Freeport Sulphur Company, assured Cuba a position as a major supplier of nickel in the world. Hotel construction from 1952-58 almost doubled the existing hotel capacity and made available numerous large and modern hotels in Havana and other major cities. In addition, numerous hotels and motels were under construction in 1958, involving a total investment in excess of $90 million and a projected capacity of 6,066 rooms. [33] Foreign tourist expenditures in Cuba increased sharply from $19 million in 1952 to a yearly average of $60 million in 1957-58. Local and foreign enterprisers clearly were mobilizing their resources in preparation for the anticipated Caribbean tourist boom of the 1960s. Two large hotels, the Habana Hilton and the Habana Riviera, figured importantly in the island's capacity to accommodate tourists seeking first class service. Cuban agricultural diversification gained momentum after 1952 and was reflected in gains in exports of farm and livestock products other than sugar and its by-products and in a respectable increase in agricultural production for domestic consumption. Rice production, advancing from 118,000 tons in 1951 to 261,000 tons in 1957, was a notable case of foreign exchange savings.

Given the nature of the international sugar market and Cuba's substantial share as a world exporter, * the nation's policymakers perceived that the sugar sector no longer could provide the stimulus for a further expansion of the economy. As a consequence, the government organized a number of development banks and passed the Industrial Promotion Law of 1953, which granted, among other things,

---

*The island produced approximately 15 percent of the global production and supplied one-third of the sugar sold in the international market. See Cuban Economic Research Project, "Cuba's Foreign Trade Before and After 1958," University of Miami, September 1962 (unpublished manuscript).

tax incentives to new industries. The implementation of these policy measures, together with a more aggressive use of the 1927 tariff, launched the Cuban economy on a new growth path through import substitution for the home market.

Industrial diversification gained momentum in the 1950s with particularly sharp increases registered from 1952-57 in the output of cement (56 percent), rubber tires (66 percent), and chemical fertilizers (46 percent).[34] Production of electric energy grew at a cumulative annual rate of 10.6 percent from 1952-57. Rapid advances also were made in the manufacture of paper from bagasse, in flour milling, the dairy products industry, and, as we have noted, Cuba achieved self-sufficiency in petroleum refining by the end of 1959. In its review of Cuba's economy, the U.N. Economic Commission for Latin America observed that a significant number of projects were underway in 1957.

> The purpose of these investment programs in the manu-
> facturing sector is to make Cuba completely self-sufficient
> at an early date in cement, tires and tubes, glass
> containers, aluminum sheet and copper wire and cables,
> and relatively self-sufficient in light steel products. . . .[35]

In addition to sugar mills and many traditional light industries, Cuba had in 1958 an impressive complex of intermediate capital goods industries producing sulphuric acid, fertilizer, cement, light steel products, paper, rubber products, glass, nickel, and petroleum products. American enterprise and technology played a decisive role in the development and growth of these intermediate capital goods industried. For example, Cuba's steel mill, Antillana de Acero, was mounted and operated with the technical assistance of the Republic Steel Corporation.

The accelerated capitalization of the Cuban economy in sectors other than sugar production is reflected in the changing composition of imports. The purchase abroad of fixed capital goods climbed steeply from less than $100 million (20 percent of total imports) in 1953 to $207 million annually (27 percent of imports) during the two years 1957-58.[36] These data and the preceding discussion suggest that Cuba in the 1950s made important gains in diminishing its dependency on the sugar sector.

THE IMPACT OF U.S. INVESTMENTS

In evaluating the role of foreign direct investment how does one cast up the balance sheet of advantages and disadvantages?[37] Basically, the host country gains a net benefit whenever a foreign enterprises adds more to the value of national output than it appropriates through its earnings. Direct benefits accrue to domestic labor (higher real wages), to consumers (lower prices), and to government (expanded revenue). If the investment is product improving or product innovating, consumers may then enjoy better quality products, or new products. Foreign investment may also allow a larger labor force to be employed (by tapping unemployed or underemployed workers) and expand the stock of natural resources (through discovery and development of mineral deposits). Finally, the foreign-owned company may generate external economies that raise production external to it, but which it cannot appropriate. Typical examples of externalities are the free provision of technical assistance to suppliers and customer firms and the systematic training of workers, technicians, and managers—only to lose this "human capital" whenever these individuals seek employment in other enterprises.

A comprehensive survey of the impact of U.S. business investments on foreign countries, including Cuba, was issued by the U.S. Department of Commerce in 1960.[38] Among other things, the survey revealed the extent to which the U.S. firms participated in the Cuban economy through production of their subsidiaries and branches for the island's market and exports. Total sales of the Cuban subsidiaries and branches of U.S. companies exceeded $700 million in 1957 (see Table 2.2). These reveal a wide sector distribution within the Cuban economy, including agriculture ($310 million), manufacturing (about $150 million), public utility services (about $130 million), and petroleum products (nearly $120 million). Except for agricultural sales (of which $250 million were for export markets) and sales of the nickel mining firms, the overwhelming shares of the output of the U.S. manufacturing, petroleum, and public utility firms were directed to the Cuban national Market.

Total sales of $729 million less company purchases of materials and supplies, $402 million, yield a figure of $327 million—the value added to the Cuban economy in 1957 by U.S. enterprises. We should deduct from this value an allowance for net production that would have occurred in the absence of the capital and organization provided by the U.S. enterprises. Considering (1) the existence of substantial unemployment in the Cuban economy and (2) the inability of Cuban entrepreneurs to engage in large scale mineral development, it is reasonable to conclude that a large proportion of value added can be attributed to U.S. direct investments.

The U.S. subsidiaries in Cuba employed an estimated 160,000 persons in 1957; and out of 2,000 supervisory, professional, and technical personnel, less than 500 were sent from the United States.[39] Foreign subsidiaries were cited by the World Bank Mission as "among those employers who pay the highest wages and who, for the most part,

TABLE 2.2

Impact of U. S. Investments in Cuba: Sales, Current Purchases,
Value Added, and Earnings, By Economic Sector, 1957
(millions of U. S. dollars)

Sector	A Sales	B Purchase of Materials and Supplies	C Value Added (A - B)	D Earnings
Agriculture	310	174	136	39
Manufacturing	149	95	54	9
Public utilities	129	31	98	12
Petroleum	118	87	31	4
Other	20	12	8	9
All industries	729	402	327	73

Source: U. S. Department of Commerce, Office of Business Economics,
U. S. Business Investments in Foreign Countries. (Washington, D. C.: Government
Printing Office, 1960), derived from tables 22, 30, and 38 (pp. 110, 118, and 127,
respectively).

TABLE 2.3

Earnings of U. S. Direct Investments in Cuba, 1951-60
(millions of U. S. dollars)

	Investments, End of Previous Year	Net Earnings*	Rate of Return (percent)
1951	642	64	9.9
1952	672	53	7.8
1953	686	30	4.3
1954	686	35	5.1
1955	713	45	6.3
1956	736	51	6.9
1957	777	73	9.3
1958	849	46	5.4
1959	879	28	3.1
1960	956	0	0.0

*Earnings are defined as the sum of the U. S. share in the net earnings (or
losses) of foreign corporations and branch profits after foreign taxes but before U. S.
taxes.

Source: U. S. Department of Commerce, Survey of Current Business, August
or September issues, 1955-61.

67956

scrupulously observe Cuba's labor legislation. . . . "[40] Though employing only seven percent of Cuba's labor force, the U. S. companies in 1957 accounted for one-third of the nation's merchandise export earnings and a little under one-fifth of total government revenues. In the opinion of Enrique V. Menocal, Premier Castro's first director of internal revenue (1 January to 1 October 1959), the U. S. corporations in Cuba were also scrupulous in meeting their tax obligations in the host country. Reflecting on his experience during those nine months, he writes,

> Not a single American contributor, whether individual or company, found it necessary to use this law (Law of Fiscal Amnesty) to mediate rectification of civilian tax statements. The Americans were almost the only ones who had contributed to the national treasury in strict conformity with national legislation. . . .[41]

The U. S. firms operating in Cuba also made critical contributions to the nation's balance of payments position in 1957 through export earnings ($273 million), net capital inflows ($88 million), and foreign exchange saved through import substitution ($130 million). Offsetting these contributions were income remittances plus fees and royalties (totaling $56 million) and imports (other than imports of trading companies or of petroleum to be processed in Cuba) amounting to roughly $100 million. On this calculation, U. S. companies accounted for a net foreign exchange gain or saving to Cuba on the order of $335 million.

The economic cost to Cuba of U. S. business holdings, measured by the rate of return (profit) on equity investment, appeared to be low when compared with U. S. direct investments in the rest of Latin America, in other parts of the world, and at home. Earnings for the 1950-59 decade (see Table 2. 3) averaged $48 million annually, or 5. 8 percent of book investment, and less than two percent of Cuba's gross national product. The belief shared by a number of otherwise well-informed scholars of Latin American affairs[42] that profits on U. S. investments in Cuba prior to the revolution were relatively high and not reinvested simply is not borne out by the available evidence.

THE PROCESS OF "CUBANIZATION"

Direct investments of U. S. companies in Cuba whose book value (net assets) approached $1 billion at the end of 1959 represented an important participation in the nation's stock of productive capital.[43] Cuba ranked second in Latin America (behind Venezuela) in the value of U.S. direct investments in 1959 and, at the moment of expropriation in 1960, they constituted one-eighth of total American investments in the area. The participation of U.S. investments in the structure of the Cuban economy in the latter 1950s was considerable, as indicated by the following approximate shares: electric power and telephone service (90 percent), raw sugar production (37 percent), commercial banking (30 percent), public service railways (50 percent), petroleum refining (66 percent), insurance (20 percent), and nickel mining (100 percent).[44]

Notwithstanding these large U.S. equity holdings in Cuba, it is very important to observe that private Cuban groups succeeded in winning control over economic activities formerly dominated by U.S. and other foreign investors. The outstanding cases are sugar, banking, air transport, and insurance.

From the 1930s on, Cubans purchased a large number of sugar mills from the U.S., Canadian, Spanish, Dutch, and French interests.* As Table 2.4 shows, the U.S. share of Cuban sugar production declined from 63 percent in 1926, to 55 percent in 1939, and 37 percent in 1958. Other foreign investors, whose sugar mills produced 42 percent of Cuba's sugar in 1926, had sold virtually all of their holdings by 1958. The divestiture of sugar mills by foreign enterprises was accompanied by the transfer of cane land to Cuban ownership. Significantly, the small farmers grew only nine percent of Cuba's cane in 1932, but by 1958 their share was well over 50 percent.[45] In consequence, Cuban capital controlled three-fourths of the sugar mills; and these, in turn, accounted for 62 percent of the island's sugar production in 1958. Local business interests, whose share of Cuba's sugar production had been reduced to a mere 22 percent in 1939, thus regained their position of dominance after the war.

The decade ending in 1955 also witnessed the return of Cuban-owned banks to a position of dominance, a position that had been lost in the crash of 1920-21 when 20 banks were forced to close their doors. As late as 1939, the foreign branch banks, mainly U.S. and Canadian, held 83 percent of all deposits; by the end of 1955 Cuban-owned banks held 60 percent of the nation's deposits. From 1939-55, the share of the Cuban companies in the insurance business increased from 38 percent to about one-half. A majority of the stock in the

---

*From 1934-51, Cubans purchased 32 mills from U.S. interests for about $35 million; nine from Canadians for $7,750,000 and two each from Spanish, Dutch, and French interests for a total of about $5 million. During the period of 1952-55, inclusive, five mills came under Cuban control. U.S. Department of Commerce, Investment in Cuba (Washington, D.C.: Government Printing Office, 1956), p. 37, footnote 16.

TABLE 2.4

Cuba: Sugar Mills and Production According to Nationality
of Ownership or Control

Nationality	1926		1939		1958	
	Number of Mills	Output (percent)	Number of Mills	Output (percent)	Number of Mills	Output (percent)
Cuba	101	n.a.*	56	22.4	131	62.1
United States	41	63.0	66	55.1	36	36.7
Other foreigners	42	n.a.	52	22.5	4	1.2
Total	184	100.0	174	100.0	161	100.0

*Not available

Note: A number of the corporations classified as U.S.-owned had Cuban stockholders.

Source: For 1926, U.S. Department of Commerce, Investment in Cuba (Washington, D.C.: Government Printing Office, 1956), p. 37, table 20. For 1939 and 1958, Anuario Azucarero, Havana, 1959.

leading air transport company, Compania Cubana de Aviacion, originally a wholly owned U. S. subsidiary, eventually passed into Cuban hands.[46] Transfer of these foreign-held assets to Cuban ownership was accomplished through normal business channels and procedures—a manifestation of the progressive maturation of the island's business community and postwar prosperity.

SUMMARY AND CONCLUSIONS

On the eve of the Cuban Revolution, the island had an essentially semideveloped, semiindustrialized market economy with a strong orientation toward the United States—its principal trading partner and external source of developmental capital. Cuba ranked third or fourth in socioeconomic welfare among the 20 Latin American nations. The nation's relatively high standard of living was, in turn, the product of a comparatively favorable endowment of human, natural, and capital resources.

U. S. business investments contributed significantly to Cuba's economic posture since the turn of the century. From the Spanish-American War in 1898 through 1929, U. S. direct investments in Cuba were concentrated in public services (railways, electric power, and communications) and in the dominant export industry—sugar. The expansion and modernization of Cuba's sugar industry under U. S. private initiative in the 1920s gave the island a competitive edge in the world sugar economy.

After the Second World War new investments by U. S.-controlled affiliates assumed a highly diversified pattern and flowed into a broad spectrum of Cuba's economic activities: infrastructure, manufacturing and commerce, petroleum refining, diversified agriculture, mining, and the tourist industry. The augmented production capabilities represented by U. S. subsidiaries and branches in Cuba were directed primarily to meet the requirements of the local market. U. S. business investments both stimulated and responded to the postwar expansion of Cuba's economy. The managerial and technical infusions associated with these investments were notably instrumental in launching Cuba on a new growth path through import substitution industrialization after 1952.

The U. S. companies contributed directly to Cuba's national income through payments of taxes and wages and salaries. They strengthened the island's balance of payments position through their exports, capital inflows, and by generating activities designed to save foreign exchange (for example, petroleum refining and general manufacturing) for the host country.

The economic cost to Cuba of U. S. business holdings, measured by the rate of return (profit) on equity investment, appeared to be low when compared with U. S. direct investments at home and abroad. The degree of penetration by U. S. investor groups into so many segments of the Cuban economy (and the domination of some) at this point in historical time was unmatched in other Latin American countries. This dependency relationship, however beneficial economically, contained a latent conflict situation. [47]

"Cubanization" proved to be a pragmatic, indigenous response to nationalist aspirations, for it was compatible with the rule of law and sustained economic growth. Had the Cuban revolution taken a different direction, we would probably have witnessed the process of "Cubanization" being extended to other sectors in which U. S. corporations exercised a dominant position: electric power, communications, and railways. The indigenous response, in contrast to the actual course of events since 1960, likely would have been made within the spirit of the 1940 constitution without alienating the United States.

NOTES

1. The historical and mainly political factors that account for the radicalization of the Cuban revolution are analyzed in two recommended scholarly works: Theodore Draper, Castro's Revolution, Myths and Realities (New York: Praeger Publishers, 1962); and Boris Goldenberg, The Cuban Revolution and Latin America (New York: Praeger Publishers, 1965), especially part II, chs. 1 and 3 and part III, chs. 2-3.

2. From the editor's introduction to Robert F. Smith, "The United States and Cuba," Marvin D. Bernstein, ed., Foreign Investment in Latin America (New York: Alfred A. Knopf, 1966), p. 145.

3. Edward Boorstein, The Economic Transformation of Cuba (New York: Monthly Review Press, 1968), pp. 2-7. Similar criticisms are given in Leo Huberman and Paul M. Sweezy, Cuba: Anatomy of a Revolution (New York: Monthly Review Press, 1961), ch. 2.

4. Maurice Zeitlin and Robert Scheer, Cuba: Tragedy in our Hemisphere (New York: Grove Press, 1963), pp. 13-29

5. James O'Connor, The Origins of Socialism in Cuba (Ithaca, N. Y.: Cornell University Press, 1970), p. 20.

6. See, for example, Gerald M. Meier, International Trade and Development (New York and Evanston: Harper and Row, 1963), pp. 5-6.

7. Henry C. Wallich, Monetary Problems of an Export Economy: The Cuban Experience, 1914-1947 (Cambridge: Harvard University Press, 1950), p. 26.

8. O'Connor, op. cit., p. 1820.

9. For example, in the five-year period from 1955-59, the U.S. price averaged 5.2 cents per pound compared with the average world price of 3.7 cents. See International Monetary Fund, Inter-national Financial Statistics, various issues, 1955-1959 (Washington, D.C.: International Monetary Fund).

10. J. Lloyd Mecham, A Survey of United States-Latin Ameri-can Relations (Boston: Houghton Mifflin Co., 1965, p. 296.

11. Ibid., p. 304.

12. U.N. Department of Social and Economic Affairs, ECLA, External Financing in Latin America, (New York: United Nations, 1965), p. 15, table 13.

13. U.S. Department of Commerce, Investment in Cuba (Washington, D.C.: Government Printing Office, 1956), p. 9.

14. Ibid., p. 35.

15. Ibid., p. 9.

16. U.N. Department of Social and Economic Affairs, op. cit., pp. 82-83.

17. U.S. Department of Commerce, op. cit., p. 10.

18. Wallich, op cit., pp. 4-5.

19. International Bank for Reconstruction and Development, Report on Cuba (Baltimore: Johns Hopkins Press, 1951), p. 72.

20. Ibid., pp. 39-40.

21. United Nations, Yearbook of National Accounts Statistics (New York: United Nations, 1962, 1963).

22. See United Nations, Statistical Handbook (New York: United Nations, 1960) and Center for Latin American Studies, Sta-tistical Abstract of Latin America (University of California at Los Angeles, 1961).

23. Benjamin Higgins, Economic Development (New York: W.W. Norton, 1968), p. 806.

24. "Some Observations on Labor Organizations in the Carib-bean" in The Caribbean: Its Economy, A. Curtis Wilgus, ed. (Gainesville: University of Florida Press, 1954), p. 167.

25. Alice Shurcliff, Labor in Cuba (Washington, D.C.: U.S. Bureau of Labor Statistics, 1957) p. 21; cited in O'Connor, op. cit., pp. 185-86.

26. Cuban Economic Research Project, Un Estudio Sobre Cuba (Miami: University of Miami Press, 1963), p. 1382.

27. "United States Foreign Investments: Measures of Growth and Economic Effects," Survey of Current Business (Septem-ber 1960): 16.

28. U.S. Department of Commerce, op. cit., p. 115, table 56.

29. Cuban Economic Research Project, A Study on Cuba (Miami: University of Miami Press, 1965), pp. 582-83.

30. The New York Times, 21 August 1960, sec. 3F.

31. Survey of Current Business (September 1965): 27, footnote to table 5.

32. Cuban Economic Research Project, op. cit., p. 549.

33. Ibid., derived from table 428, p. 569.

34. U.N. Economic Commission for Latin America: Economic Survey of Latin America, 1957 (New York: United Nations, 1959), pp. 190-93.

35. Ibid., pp. 190-91.

36. Derived from Cuban Economic Research Project, op. cit., p. 618, table 464.

37. A good framework for analysis of the impact of foreign investment is given in Gerald Meier, The International Economics of Development (New York: Harper and Row, 1968), ch. 6.

38. U.S. Department of Commerce, U.S. Business Investments in Foreign Countries (Washington, D.C.: Government Printing Office, 1960).

39. Ibid., p. 122, table 34.

40. International Bank for Reconstruction and Development, op. cit., p. 734.

41. Letter to the author from Enrique V. Menocal dated 10 October 1968. The latter is currently associate professor of economics at the Drexel Institute of Technology in Philadelphia.

42. For example, see Arpad von Lazar, Latin American Politics: A Primer (Boston: Allyn and Bacon, 1971), p. 113.

43. For an industry breakdown of invested capital see Cuban Economid Research Project, op. cit., p. 555, table 409. The capital value of Cuba's industrial plant (including the sugar industry, transportation, and communication facilities) was calculated at $3.2 billion for 1957.

44. Including the U.S. government-owned Nicaro Nickel Company.

45. O'Connor, op. cit., pp. 27-28.

46. U.N. Department of Economics and Social Affairs, Foreign Capital in Latin America (New York: United Nations, 1955), p. 80.

47. See Leland L. Johnson, "U.S. Business Interests in Cuba and the Rise of Castro," World Politics, 18, no. 2 (April 1965).

3

U.S. INVESTMENTS AND
THE MEXICAN REVOLUTION

The massive penetration of the Mexican economy by U.S., British, and other foreign direct investments prior to the 1910 revolution* generated a powerful nationalist reaction that ever since has motivated Mexico's continuing quest for "economic independence." A candid and realistic expression of the nation's attitude towards foreign investments was provided in a recent official Mexican document that stated, "A political understanding has been reached, which is capable of giving meaning to national development interests. And this is based on the conviction that sovereignty and independence have a higher value than the economic factor."[1] This statement serves to underscore the fact that Mexican public policy toward multinational corporations involves striking a delicate balance between the country's objective need for foreign investment (and the associated managerial-technological resources) and the containment of such corporations within the bounds of an acceptable role in the economic life of the nation.

---

*The available evidence suggests that, of Mexico's total accumulated investment outside of agriculture and the handicraft industries, foreign interests in 1910 accounted for two-thirds. In that year, foreigners owned 72 million acres of Mexican land, roughly one-seventh of the land surface of the country. Raymond Vernon, The Dilemma of Mexico's Development (Cambridge, Mass.: Harvard University Press, 1963), pp. 43 and 50.

THE PORFIRIAN ERA, 1877-1910

"For nearly seven decades Mexico had been in the throes of civil war of one sort or another. Its productive capacities, even to feed itself, had dropped to the lowest possible ebb. No rational men would invest in its apparent future, seemingly dedicated to continued chaos." Thus wrote the late Howard Cline,[2] one of this country's leading historians of Mexico, in describing the predicament of Mexico on the eve of Porfirio Diaz' rise to power. It is against this background that one must evaluate the policies and accomplishments of Diaz and his economic ministers (who called themselves the cientificos) in their drive to modernize Mexico.

The nation's chronic failure to meet service on the external debt during the 1850s led to foreign seizure of Mexico's Gulf ports and ultimately, occupation of the Mexican land by the forces of imperial France. To avoid recurrence of this danger, Diaz sought to put Mexico's credit on a sound basis. Second, he moved to pacify the countryside with the help of the rurales, thereby securing property against seizure or destruction. By these and other measures Diaz won for Mexico a position of respect among nations. The number of countries represented diplomatically in Mexico grew from six in 1877 to 42 in 1910. The absence of a national market and the paucity of risk capital and managerial expertise indicated Mexico's logical development path: a link-up with the industrializing nations of the world. Mexico, however, was bidding for foreign loans and investments at a time when other capital-poor lands, notably the United States, also were seeking such assistance. Mexico, consequently, had to offer more than equal attractions.

The economic policies of the Porfiriato produced three major achievements: (1) the creation of an economic infrastructure; (2) the development of an incipient national market for manufactured goods; and (3) the integration of Mexico with the international economy, including the ten-fold expansion of real exports.

Railway track mileage rose from less than 500 miles in 1877 to 15,000 miles in 1910. Radiating out of Mexico City the railway network by 1910 served most important state capitals, the leading centers of agriculture, mining, industry, and commerce and extended to ports on both oceans, the U.S. border, and the Guatemala frontier. From 1902-09, Yves Limantour, Diaz' most brilliant minister of finance, achieved his aim for national control of railways in what was to become the first "Mexicanization" of foreign investments. His plan involved organization of a new corporation, the National Railways of Mexico, in which the government held a majority of shares. The Mexican government thus obtained direct control over more than one-half of the railroad mileage and two-thirds of the lines of primary importance.[3]

Large scale investments by U.S. mining firms converted Mexico into a leading world mineral-producing country. In 1902 Mexico surpassed the United States to rank first in the output of silver, and in 1904 Mexico became second only to the United States as the most important copper-producing country in the world.

Mexico's internal market widened under the impact of the railroads and the elimination of regional import duties by constitutional amendment in 1886. Thus Mexico, in the words of Raymond Vernon, was converted "from a country of isolated little markets, chopped up by a difficult geography and by man-made trade restrictions, to one in which goods could move easily and freely."[4]

The cientificos encouraged selective immigration to Mexico, especially from France and Germany. The role of these newcomers in the formative stage of Mexico's industrial development was extraordinarily important. Most of the mechanized cotton textile plants that came into being during the Porfirian era claimed a Frenchman as a major partner, usually a dominant one. Mexico's first steel plant, Compania Fundidora de Fierro y Acero de Monterrey, was organized in 1900 by the New Yorker Eugene Kelly in a rare joint venture with key Monterrey capitalists.[5]

By 1910 Mexico had over one million industrial workers, or 19 percent of the active population.[6] During the first decade of this century, according to Placido Garcia Reynoso, former undersecretary of industry and commerce, Mexico's industrial sector "experienced substantial diversification, already counting with incipient production of iron and steel and chemicals and with significant output in food products, tobacco products, textiles, paper and construction."[7]

In the view of most historians, the impressive economic achievements of the Porfirian period carried a high social and political cost: the alienation of the traditional Indian lands and the domination of the Mexican economy by foreign investors.

THE CHANGING SECTOR PROFILE OF U.S. INVESTMENTS,
1914-72

Reflecting an earlier export-oriented stage of Mexican development, U.S. direct investments in both 1914 and 1929 were concentrated in resource-oriented activities and in public services, including railways. In those two years, U.S. investments in oil fields, mines, and plantations represented nearly three-fourths and public services about one-fourth of the total (see Table 3.1). American-controlled manufacturing and commercial investments in those years made a negligible contribution to the Mexican economy.

TABLE 3.1

U.S. Direct Investments in Mexico by Industry for Selected Years
(millions of U.S. dollars)

Industry	1914	Percent of Total	1929	Percent of Total	1946	Percent of Total	1972	Percent of Total
Agriculture	37	6.3	59	8.6	4	1.3	—	—
Mining and smelting	302	51.4	230	33.7	111	35.1	124	6.2
Petroleum	85	14.5	206	30.2	7	2.2	32	1.6
Manufacturing	10	1.7	6	0.9	66	20.9	1,385	70.0
Public services	144	24.6	164	24.0	112	35.4	a	—
Trade	4	0.7	a	—	a	—	191[b]	9.2
Other	5	0.8	18	2.6	16	5.1	260	13.0
Total	587	100.0	683	100.0	316	100.0	1,993	100.0

[a]Included in "other."

[b]Book value at end of 1969.

Sources: For 1914, see Cleoma Lewis, America's Stake in International Investments (Washington, D. C.: The Brookings Institution, 1938). For 1929-64, see U.S. Department of Commerce, U.S. Investments in Latin American Economy (Washington, D.C.: Government Printing Office, 1958), p. 180, table 102. For 1972, see Survey of Current Business (September 1973): 26-27, table 8A.

Despite the social tensions and civil warfare that character-ized the decade following the overthrow of the Diaz dictatorship, the total value of U. S. investments continued to grow. Only in the mining sector, which suffered heavy damage to machinery and equipment, did U. S. investments register a decline from 1914-29. The electric power power industry, financed initially by British and other European in-vestors, changed hands in 1928 and 1929 when the original owners sold their interests to the American and Foreign Power Company, a U. S. concern, and the Canadian-owned Mexican Light and Power Company.

American direct investments in three of Mexico's "traditional" branches of economic activity—public services, petroleum, and agri-culture—probably reached their historical peak levels in 1929, on the eve of the Great Depression. The expropriatory measures of Presi-dent Lazaro Cardenas against U. S.-owned agricultural properties (1936), railways (1937), and petroleum fields, wells, and refineries (1938) account for most of the dramatic decline of U. S. outstanding investments from 1929-46. Also, world prices of silver and indus-trial metals remained depressed throughout the 1930s; and conse-quently many U. S. mining affiliates in Mexico either went into bank-ruptcy or had to write down the value of their assets.

Examination of the sector composition of U. S. investments in Mexico viewed over the longer period 1929-72 reveals some very sig-nificant absolute and relative changes. Of major importance is the explosive growth of the U. S. stake in Mexico's manufacturing sector (from one percent to 70 percent) and commerce (from a negligible share to probably 10 percent)—both in response to the requirements of the national market. Investments in mining and smelting fell in both relative (from 34 percent to 6 percent) and absolute values. American investments in petroleum production and refining were absorbed after their expropriation by a government-owned monopoly, Petroleos Mexicanos (PEMEX), leaving only $32 million in U. S. marketing operations. Agricultural holdings of U. S. citizens south of the border have fallen sharply since 1936, and U. S. investments in public services became negligible after 1960.

Three factors account for the dramatic change in the sector composition of U. S. direct investments in Mexico: (1) economic nationalism associated with the Mexican revolution; (2) growth and change in the structure of the Mexican economy; and (3) alternative sources of external financing.

Beginning with the presidential term of Cardenas (1934-40), Mexico has added steadily to a long list of fields to which external investment is denied entry or in which foreigners must limit them-selves to a minority position. The nation's expanding, protected market along with a favorable climate for investment in manufacturing and trade has attracted a vigorous U.S. investment response along a limited front. Companies that once supplied the Mexican consumer and capital goods market by export sales from their plants in the U.S. were forced to establish production facilities in Mexico or forfeit the market as prohibitive tariffs or import restrictions were imposed on their products.* In many instances, U.S.-based multinational corporations (for example, the automotive industry) were induced to set up integrated production facilities in Mexico as the only alternative to complete exclusion from the dynamic national market.

Mexico since 1940 has undergone a sustained pace of economic growth averaging 6 percent annually for the past 30 years and 6.5 percent since the mid-1950s. This impressive advance in real output (GNP) has been led by the expansion of the industrial sector, comprising manufacturing, electric power, and construction. Manufacturing since the mid-1950s has grown at an annual rate of nearly 9 percent, spearheaded by consumer durables and capital goods production. Commerce also has been a dynamic sector in the economic growth of Mexico. The transformation of the Mexican economy since 1940 is reflected in the relative decline of the labor force in agriculture, from 65 percent in 1940 to less than 40 percent in 1972, and the growing opportunities for employment in urban activities: commerce, government service, construction, manufacturing, and trade. Since the mid-1950s, Mexico has managed to avoid serious inflation while maintaining a stable exchange rate and currency convertibility. Notwithstanding rapid population growth, Mexico's per capita real income during this period increased at a rate of nearly three percent annually, reaching nearly $700 in 1972.

The third factor, alternative sources of external financing, though of lesser importance in shaping the new pattern of U.S. investments, proved of great importance to the prospects of the Mexican petroleum industry and to public services. The U.S. Export-Import Bank, for example, has accommodated the Mexican government in financing the sale of petroleum and railway equipment. The willingness of the World Bank to provide long-term credits for the rehabilitation and expansion of economic overhead projects provided Mexico with the opportunity to nationalize its electric power and communications industries.

---

*Import policy is effectuated through two types of controls—tariffs and quantitative restrictions—formulated and administered by the executive branch of the federal government. The Ministry of Industry and Commerce has virtually unlimited authority over the granting of import licenses.

American investments in Mexican mines, petroleum fields, plantations, and railways indicates that their impact until the 1930s was diffused greatly among the several regions of Mexico. Mines and smelters managed and financed by U. S. risk capital were particullarly important in generating economic activity in Mexico's north region, mainly the states of Durango, Sonora, Zacatecas, and Chihuahua. United States, British, and Dutch petroleum company operations were located in the country's northeast and Gulf regions; and U. S. investor-owned livestock and agricultural holdings (for example, cotton, sugar, coffee, chicle) were particularly significant in the north of the country.

The profound shift of U. S. investments away from these traditional fields of economic activity to manufacturing and commerce resulted after 1940, in a high regional concentration focused on the Federal District, the neighbor State of Mexico, and, to a lesser degree, the Monterrey area. In 1965, for example, 40 percent of value added in manufacturing was accounted for by the Federal District, 16 percent by the State of Mexico, and 10 percent by Nuevo Leon, which includes the city of Monterrey. These three places thus accounted for two-thirds of the value added in manufacturing and 55 percent of the sector's employment. [8]

THE IMPACT OF U. S. INVESTMENTS: BENEFITS AND COSTS

It is clear that the total qualitative benefit of U. S. investments to the Mexican economy has been higher in the postwar period than in earlier times. The level of skills and technical knowledge transferred to Mexico per dollar of constant purchasing power invested undoubtedly has increased. Relative to former times, a much larger share of U. S. investment has gone into manufacturing and commerce, where joint ownership of subsidiaries, efforts to obtain better quality goods from local suppiers, and emulation by local competitors tend to spur the tranference of technical knowledge and skills. Significantly, half of the U. S. manufacturing subsidiaries operating in Mexico at the end of 1967 were joint ventures, as compared with 30 percent in 1957 and only 19 percent in 1939;[9] and U. S. subsidiaries in all activities now train and employ a much higher percentage of Mexicans in technical and administrative positions than before World War II. For another thing, the share of the total value of goods produced by U. S. affiliates that is retained in one form or another in Mexico has also increased.

Bank of Mexico data help clarify the role of external capital resources, particularly foreign direct investment, in Mexico's economy. [10] From 1960-70 foreign direct investments (including reinvested profits) contributed 6.1 percent of gross internal savings and 7.6 percent of gross private investment. Capital consumption (depreciation allowances) of foreign-owned affiliates are not included; hence, the contribution of foreign direct investment to the nation's gross internal savings appears to be underestimated. The annual growth rate of foreign direct investment flow in the period 1960-70 (15.2 percent) surpassed that of private investment (12.3 percent) and total fixed gross investment (12.2 percent). American-controlled enterprises in Mexico accounted for about 80 percent of the accumulated foreign direct investment in this period: U.S. affiliates in Mexico dominate automobiles, electrical consumer goods, food processing, pharmaceuticals, and, until 1973, tobacco products. They also hold considerable investments in commerce—Sears, for example, has 22 Mexican branches—and in tourism.

The recently published monograph Impact of Foreign Investment in Mexico is a thoroughly documented and objective study of the history and role of foreign enterprise in Mexico. This joint work of Herbert K. May, consultant to the Council of the Americas, and Jose Antonio Fernandez Arena, dean of the Faculty of Commerce and Administration of the National Autonomous University of Mexico, draws on the most recent information developed by the U.S. Department of Commerce on the Mexican operations of U.S. business firms. The authors shed valuable light on the highly controversial subject of the balance of payments effects of foreign investments on the host country. [11] The study shows that in the period 1965-68, U.S.-controlled firms made vital contributions to Mexico's balance of payments position through average annual export earnings of $446 million, net capital inflow of $106 million, and foreign exchange savings of $1,305 million mainly through import substitution (the authors estimate that the sales prices of goods produced by Mexican subsidiaries of U.S. companies were, on the average, one-third higher than the cost in foreign exchange of importing comparable products would have been). The U.S. affiliates contributed no less than 38 percent of Mexico's total exports in 1966. On the other side of the ledger were average annual income remittances plus fees and royalties (totaling $116 million) and import costs of production averaging $190 million per year. On the basis of this calculation, Mexican subsidiaries of U.S. firms accounted for an average net balance of payments support to Mexico of $1,552 million annually.

Mexico's sulphur reserves were increased dramatically by the exploratory and development efforts of two U.S.-controlled mining enterprises, Pan American Sulphur and Texas Gulf Sulphur. Before they were "Mexicanized" in 1967, these U.S. affiliates raised Mexico's sulphur output from negligible quantities in the 1940s to over 1.7 million metric tons in 1964.

Sales by U.S. manufacturing subsidiaries in Mexico rose from $643 million in 1957 to $1,480 million in 1966, a 130 percent increase.[12] During the latter year the emphasis was on high technology, capital intensive types of industries: chemical and allied products ($405 million), transportation equipment ($281 million), machinery ($265 million), fabricated metals ($117 million). U.S. manufacturing subsidiaries were also significantly involved in the production of food products ($148 million). They employed a total of 101,335 persons in 1966 and their managerial staffs numbered 4,642 people, of whom only 390 (8.6 percent) were U.S. employees. Their technical and professional staffs totalled 9,528 persons, of whom 86 (less than one percent) were from the parent companies.

The Border Industrialization Program and the associated investments by U.S. affiliates constitute an important regionally focused effort within the 1,900-mile-long and 12-mile-deep border zone. The idea of encouraging U.S. firms to establish plants within this border zone was first advanced in May 1965 by Octaviano Campos Sales, Mexico's former secretary of industry and commerce, following a trip to the Far East.[13] The Mexican government conceived of the border zone as "an alternative to Hong Kong, Japan, and Puerto Rico" in the location of assembly plants. American manufacturing affilates are permitted to import equipment and materials into the border zone duty free. To benefit from these provisions, including duty-free exports, the U.S.-owned plants must locate within the zone; and they cannot sell their products in the Mexican market. When entering the U.S. market, the products of these plants are taxed only on the value added in Mexico rather than their full value.

Since the initiation of the investment incentive program in mid-1966, 426 assembly plants (mostly U.S. owned) have been established in the border zone.[14] They provided employment directly for 58,000 persons and generated indirectly an estimated 100,000 additional jobs in the region.[15] Most of the operations are in precision, labor intensive industries such as electronics, which accounts for 40 percent of total value added, and apparel factories, which account for 30 percent of border zone production.

The Mexican border zone, separated from the rest of the nation by desert and mountains, comprised a number of essentially nonindustrial cities. The flow of U.S. direct investments into this region since the mid-1960s makes an important contribution toward solving the serious unemployment problem in the urban zone that extends from Tijuana in the west to Matamoros in the east. It also indicates a significant initiative in the geographical dispersion of manufacturing activity in Mexico.

The economic cost to Mexico of U.S. business holdings, measured by the rate of return (profit) on equity investment, appeared to be low when compared with U. S. direct investments in the rest of Latin America and in other parts of the world. Profits earned on U. S. investments in Mexico (before U. S. taxes) averaged only 8. 6 percent annually during 1960-69, as compared with 13. 2 percent in the rest of Latin America. [16] The rate of return in mining and smelting during the 1960s was particularly unfavorable for Mexico (12. 6 percent) in comparison with the region (21. 3 percent).

"THE RECONQUEST OF MEXICO FOR MEXICANS"

The keystone of Mexican foreign investment policy after 1910 became, in the words of Ramon Beteta, former undersecretary for foreign affairs, "the reconquest of Mexico for Mexicans."[17] Consequently, every Mexican president since the revolution, as Harry K. Wright observes, "has emphasized economic independence as a fundamental principle, and most have gone on record as viewing foreign investment with some degree of caution. [18] The result has been that, one by one, sectors of the Mexican economy that were initially developed by foreign risk capital and technology—oil, agriculture, railways, public utilities, and mining—have been closed entirely or partially to foreigners (see Table 3. 2). Some Mexican Presidents, notably Manuel Avila Camacho (December 1940-November 1946) and Miguel Aleman (December 1946-November 1952) assumed a moderate, even friendly posture in relation to foreign investors. Others, for example, Lazaro Cardenas (December 1934-November 1940), Adolfo Lopez Mateos (December 1958-November 1964), and Luis Echevarria Alverez (December 1970-) changed the ground rules by which the foreign investor operated in Mexico.

The constitution of 1917 was the legal expression of a new social, political, and economic philosophy. Among the most important economic articles were those that sought agrarian reform, the abolition of monopolies, and the protection of labor, as well as the establishment of government title to subsoil mineral deposits (article 27). In its many facets the Queretaro Constitution, as it is commonly called, was tinged with an antiforeign complexion and epitomized the spirit of Mexican nationalism.

Aggressive implementation of the constitution of 1917 did not begin until the inauguration of President Cardenas in December 1934. During his six-year term the economic phase of the revolution reached its greatest momentum. The framework for this program was the Six-Year Plan, which aimed at extending agrarian reform, broadening labor legislation, and bringing under government ownership and control petroleum and other critical industries of the nation. The dramatic changes in the foreigners' stake in Mexico that occurred during

TABLE 3.2

Expropriation, Nationalization, and "Mexicanization"
of U.S. Direct Investments, 1903–73

Year	Industry	Nature of Acquisition	Companies Affected
1903–09	Railways	"Mexicanization"	Mexican Central Railway and other companies
1936	Agriculture	Expropriation	Plantations and livestock companies
1937	Railways	Expropriation	Remaining railroad companies
1938	Petroleum	Expropriation	Standard Oil (N.J.), Sinclair Oil Co., several others
1958	Telephones	"Mexicanization"	ITT
1960	Electric power	Nationalization	American and Foreign Power Co.
1961–72	Mining	"Mexicanization"	American Metal Climax
			American Smelting and Refining Corp.
			Pan American Sulphur
			Texas Gulf Sulphur
			Anaconda Co.
1973	Tobacco	"Mexicanization"	Liggett and Myers, Inc.

Source: Compiled by author.

those eventful years are borne out statistically: from a value exceeding $1.5 billion in 1935, foreign direct investments fell to $480 million in 1940—a contraction of more than two-thirds (see Table 3.3). In 1935, the year preceding the expropriatory actions by Cardenas, U.S. direct investments in politically sensitive industries were calculated by the Brookings Institution.[19]

Petroleum	$206.0 million
Railways	60.5 million
Agriculture	35.7 million

A rough estimate, then, would put the value of all expropriated properties belonging to U.S. citizens at over $300 million.

TABLE 3.3

Foreign Direct Investments in Mexico by Industrial Groups,
1935 and 1940
(in millions of U.S. dollars)

Industry	1935	1940
Mining and smelting	396.3	186.0
Railroads	196.4	—[a]
Rural holdings	178.5	14.0
Oil lands and refineries	381.5	—
Public utilities	196.4	246.0[b]
Manufacturing	48.4	20.0
Bank shares	—	—
Wholesale and retail	87.0	9.0
Miscellaneous	25.2	5.0
Total	1509.7	480.0

[a]Included in public utility group.

[b]Includes railroads and other transportation.

Sources: For 1935, U.S. Tariff Commission, Agricultural, Pastoral, and Forest Industries of Mexico (Washington, D.C.: Government Printing Office, 1940), p. 24. For 1940, U.S., Congress, House, Committee on Interstate and Foreign Commerce, Fuel Investigation: Mexican Petroleum, 80th Cong., 2d sess., 1949, p. 81.

Between May 1940 and April 1942, Mexico reached agreements with the U. S. oil companies for the settlement of their outstanding claims (see the next section of this chapter). The agrarian and general claims of U. S. citizens against Mexico, arising principally from the 1936 land expropriations, were settled in 1941 for $40 million, including accrued interest.[20] In April 1948 the Mexican government offered bondholders of the National Railway Bonds (which had been in default prior to the 1937 expropriation) compensation for the reitrement of their bonds. About 37 percent of the railway bonds were held by British interests and 30 percent by U. S. investors, with the remaining outstanding issues divided principally among Frenchmen, Belgians, and Germans.[21] In choosing either option, the bondholders accepted a very substantial reduction from the nominal principal amounts of the bonds and a large reduction in interest payments.

Following a period of stability in the "rules of the game, " from 1940-60, efforts to replace foreign control over certain branches of the Mexican economy with native ownership again became manifest. During the presidential term of Lopez Mateos, the foreign-controlled electric power companies were nationalized and the "Mexicanization" of foreign-controlled mining enterprises was initiated.

In 1958, a group of Mexican financiers, led by the late Carlos Trouyet, acquired a controlling interest in Telefonos de Mexico, a company that had been jointly owned by ITT and the L. M. Ericson group of Sweden. By taking the initiative in "Mexicanizing" the nation's telephone system, Trouyet assured that the company for the time being would remain a privately owned rather than a governmental utility. However, in 1972, in accordance with President Echeverria's aim to increase the direct role of the Mexican state within the economy, Telefonos de Mexico passed from private to public control.

The Federal Electricity Commission (CFE), created by the government in 1937, extended federal authority to all phases of Mexico's power industry and by 1960, CFE's share of the nation's total electric power capacity had reached 40 percent. Meanwhile, the foreign-owned power companies whose rates were controlled by CFE were unable to generate sufficient profits to expand their capacity in response to the burgeoning industrial and residential demand for electricity. With rate adjustments lagging far behind rising money costs of electricity generation and distribution, company profits averaged an insignificant 1. 5 percent of their investments during the period 1939-58.[22] A new coalition of consumers and small industrialists grouped around the National Chamber of Manufacturing Industries (CNIT), using its political influence during the postwar year to attach the foreign-owned utility companies, whom they blamed for deteriorating electric power service. The solution came in 1960 when Mexican officials approached American and Foreign Power Company with a proposition to sell its holdings. Later that year the Mexican government purchased outright the holdings of American and Foreign Power and 90 percent of the outstanding common and preferred stock of the Mexican Light and Power Company, a Canadian subsidiary.

After nationalization, the Mexican government granted itself what it would not give to the U.S. and Canadian electric power enterprises: a substantial rate increase. By allowing the power industry to operate again at a profitable level, Mexican officials were able to convince the World Bank that it should finance the $130 million foreign exchange component of a four-year electrification expansion program.

President Adolfo Lopez Mateos announced that the book value of the two companies, totaling 3,375 million pesos, was acquired by the state for 650 million pesos,[23] less than one-fifth of total value! Apparently, the foreign-controlled power companies, squeezed between rising money costs and fixed rates, had little choice but to dispose of their assets at bargain basement prices.

In its original and moderate connotation, the "Mexicanization" policy refers to the effort of inducing a foreign enterprise to sell an important part, preferably a majority, of its stock to Mexicans. "Mexicanization" has also come to mean, in both language and action, the transfer of 100 percent foreign ownership and control to Mexicans, private or public. Well-to-do Mexican entrepreneurs generally have favored the first interpretation cited above, particularly in the mining industry. They have been eager to stake their claim, with the help of their government, in a profitable enterprise—after the foreign investor has provided both the venture capital and advanced technology and has borne the initial risk.

The "Mexicanization" policy has been implemented through the application of both penalties and incentives. Reluctance on the part of a foreign affiliate to surrender majority ownership to Mexican interests could result in discriminatory taxation, lowering of production quotas, diversion of government contracts, and the withholding of business operation permits and import licenses.[24]

A willingness of a foreign investor to yield to "Mexicanization" normally has received sympathetic reaction from the government in the form of tax benefits and other inducements. Union Carbide Mexicana, S.A., thus found it advantageous in 1961 to sell 40 percent of its shares, the first true public offering of a foreign company on the Mexican stock exchange. Subsequent offerings by Union Carbide, used to expand its Mexican operations, further served to increase Mexican participation in the company's stock. Anderson Clayton, John Deere and Fruehauf, among others in a growing number of Mexican affiliates of U.S. firms, have also "gone public."

"Mexicanization" of the nonferrous mining and processing industry was initiated with the Mining Law of 1961. This law, implementing article 27 of the constitution, provided that only firms with a majority of Mexican capital may obtain new mining concessions. In the exploitation of government-owned reserves, Mexican participation must represent not less than 66 percent of the corporate capital. To provide an incentive for "Mexicanization," the mining tax code was revised in 1963 to allow any company to obtain a production and export tax reduction of 50-75 percent, with a 50 percent decrease being automatic on "Mexicanization."[25] Metalurgica Mexicana Penoles (a subsidiary of American Metal Climax) was the first major U.S.-owned mining enterprise to be "Mexicanized." A group of Mexican private investors acquired 51 percent of the subsidiary's stock in 1961 and purchased the remaining 49 percent in 1965. In that same year, the Mexican government and Mexican private investors jointly acquired a controlling interest in ASARCO Mexicana, S.A., an affiliate of the American Smelting and Refining Company.

The sulphur mining industry, which had been completely dominated by affiliates of Pan American Sulphur and Texas Gulf Sulphur, yielded to "Mexicanization" in 1967. Initially, the Mexican government acquired 34 percent and a group of Mexican private investors (Banco Nacional de Mexico, Isaac Bussudo Perez, and others), 23 percent of Azufrera Panamericana's stock. Pan American retained 34 percent of the stock and agreed to provide management and technical assistance to the newly organized joint venture. However, in 1972 the Mexican government, through Nacional Financiera, purchased the remaining U.S. interest, thereby acquiring through majority ownership of the company control over three-fourths of the nation's sulphur production and one-half of its sulphur reserves.

Anaconda's wholly owned Mexican subsidiary, Compania Minera de Cananea, S.A., was the last major operation left in the hands of foreigners. Expansion of the Cananea mine had been ruled out because of the prohibitive production and export taxes imposed on foreign-controlled mining enterprises. "Mexicanization" by agreement, in which governmental agencies purchased 26 percent and private investors 25 percent of the stock, opened the door in 1973 for a major expansion program. Production at the Cananea open-pit copper mine, in which Anaconda retains 49 percent of the stock, reached 45,000 tons of copper in 1973 and is scheduled to increase to 70,000 tons annually by 1976.[26]

In the mining sector, the "Mexicanization" policy achieved notable success. During the latter 1950s, between 80 and 90 percent of the country's output of gold, silver, copper, lead, zinc, and antimony was in the hands of U.S.-controlled enterprises; similarly, 100 percent of Mexico's sulphur, bismuth, cadmium, and arsenic were

mined by U. S. affiliates.[27] After the "Mexicanization" of major
U. S.-controlled mining and smelting enterprises, 98 percent of the
value of Mexico's mining production at the end of 1973 originated in
nationally controlled enterprises.

The ground rules for multinational companies doing business
in Mexico were again changed by the Law to Promote Mexican Investment and to Regulate Foreign Investment, enacted in March 1973. The
new legislation defines activities that are reserved exclusively to the
state and to Mexican firms and places limits on the investment of
foreign capital.[28] It lays down specific rules and conditions to be
observed by foreign investment and establishes the principle of
majority participation by Mexican capital. It also for the first time
places restrictions on the sale of national firms to investors from
other countries. Article 8 limits the acquisition by foreigners of more
than 25 percent of the capital or more than 49 percent of the fixed
assets of an established Mexican business enterprise. It also insures
that the management of an established Mexican enterprise does not
come under the control of a foreign investor.

Activities that are reserved exclusively for the state include
petroleum and basic petrochemicals, electric power, railroads, and
telegraph and wireless communications. Reserved exclusively for
Mexicans or Mexican companies are the following: radio and tele-
vision, urban and interurban transportation and federal highway transport, domestic air and maritime transportation, forestry exploitation,
and gas distribution. Other activities from which foreigners are not
excluded require a majority of Mexican capital in varying percentages.
The National Commission on Foreign Investment, created by the law,
is empowered to decide on the exceptions to the 49 percent maximum
foreign participation in accordance with the economic policy criteria
established in the legislation itself. Significantly, one of the two
basic purposes of the new law is to "consolidate the country's
economic independence."[29] President Echeverria, under whose
direction the law was enacted, has also moved to increase the direct
role of the state within the Mexican economy and has projected his
image as a leader of the "third world" against "Yanquee imperialism."[30]

THE OIL EXPROPRIATION CONTROVERSY

To stimulate foreign venture capital into the development of
the petroleum and mining industries, Diaz and his cientificos altered
the nation's legal system that previously had maintained the inalienable patrimony of the crown (that is, the nation) in subsoil

resources.* The Mining Codes of 1884 and 1892 and the law of 1909, following the Napoleonic Code, reversed the traditional Mexican position giving the surface owner exclusive property rights over pools or deposits of mineral fuels in all their forms and varieties.[31]

The constitution of 1917 abandoned the principle of ownership of the subsoil by the surface owner and provided for strict separation of rights to the subsoil from surface rights. Article 27 stipulates that the nation has direct ownership of petroleum and all solid, liquid, or gaseous hydrocarbons—as well as metals and precious stones. This article further provides that "expropriation may be effected only for reasons of public utility and by means of indemnification."[32] Article 27 of the new constitution thus raised an important question regarding the status of oil rights acquired by foreigners prior to 1917 under the mining laws of 1884, 1892, and 1909. This was to become the focus of the ensuing legal and diplomatic conflict involving Mexico, the foreign-controlled oil companies, and the governments of the United States and England.

Commercial oil production in Mexico was initiated in 1901 by Edward L. Doheny, an American entrepreneur, in the Huasteca fields located within the Tampico-Tuxpan region. Doheny's Huasteca Petroleum Company was subsequently purchased by the Standard Oil Company of New Jersey. Mexican oil production eventually became concentrated among the "Big Three:" Mexican Eagle Company ("El Aguila"), a subsidiary of the Royal-Dutch Shell group, the Huasteca Petroleum Company, now a subsidiary of Standard Oil, and the Sinclair Company. On the eve of expropriation, the Mexican Eagle and Huasteca groups were in control of more than 70 percent of Mexico's crude production (60 percent and 12 percent, respectively, in 1936).[33]

Production increased rapidly and reached an historical peak of 193 million barrels in 1921, more than 25 percent of the world's total oil output. In that year Mexico became (after the United States) the second largest oil-producing nation. Oil production accounted for 7 percent of the nation's GNP and a substantial share of her exports. After 1921 petroleum output decreased until the beginning of the Second World War. The prevailing uncertainty as to the status of the oil companies was probably the most important factor conditioning this downward trend, although labor troubles and failure of large wells were also contributory causes.

---

*Oil was specifically enumerated in the Laws of the Indies as one of the resources that were inalienable property reserved to the Spanish Crown. When Mexico achieved independence from Spain, she inherited the Spanish legal position regarding the status of oil and other minerals.

In 1921 the Mexican Supreme Court ruled that the 1917 constitution was not retroactive with respect to petroleum rights acquired prior to the adoption of the constitution, provided "positive acts" had been performed in exercising such rights. [34] Following this decision, negotiations ensued between the governments of Mexico and the United States that culminated in the so-called Bucareli Conference of 1923. This conference was held for the purpose of finding a basis on which the U. S. government could recognize the government of President Alvaro Obregon. One of the outcomes of the conference was an agreement in which the Mexican government agreed that the owners of lands acquired prior to 1 May 1917 who had performed "positive acts" indicating their intention to exploit the oil resources were to be granted confirmatory concessions. [35]

Two years following the Bucareli Conference, the Mexican Congress, under the initiative of President Plutarco Calles, enacted the petroleum law of 26 December 1925. In its original form, this law required the foreign oil companies to exchange their subsoil titles of unlimited duration for 50-year concessions. The American government protested that the new legislation was retroactive, confiscatory, and that it violated the agreement reached at the Bucareli Conference. Extended negotiations between the able U. S. Ambassador Dwight W. Morrow and President Calles, however, again led to an amicable settlement of the petroleum question. The Mexican Supreme Court on 17 November 1927 declared unconstitutional those provisions of the 1925 petroleum law that required companies to exchange their titles of ownership for 50-year concessions. [36] Thereupon, the congress, at the suggestion of President Calles, amended the law to validate in perpetuity all titles obtained prior to 1 May 1917 provided, of course, that there was evidence of performance of "positive acts." [37] This compromise removed from discussion the most serious cause of contention between the United States and Mexico.

With the inauguration of President Lazaro Cardenas on 30 November 1934, the status of foreign investments, particularly in the petroleum and agricultural sectors, again became critical. The Expropriation Law of 1936, in conjunction with new labor legislation, enabled the Cardenas administration to exert the necessary pressure to create a "labor squeeze" on foreign-owned petroleum, mining, and agricultural enterprises. Unions were organized and supported by Cardenas in their demand for greatly increased wages and fringe benefits. The president also was able to assure that the judicial system inevitably would find in favor of the workers when cases came to court.

The oil workers were organized on an industry-wide basis, the Union of Petroleum Workers, which then affiliated with the Confederation of Mexican Workers. Thus organized and with government support, the union in November 1936 confronted the major oil companies with demands for wage increases and social welfare benefits. Concession to these proposals would have augmented the annual labor costs of the companies by 65 million _pesos_, an increase of more than 100 percent. [38] When the companies indicated their inability to comply with these demands, the petroleum workers went on strike on 27 May 1937. During the strike, the oil companies agreed to increase their annual labor bill by about 20 million _pesos_, an offer that the union rejected. The dispute was then submitted to the Federal Conciliation and Arbitration Board, and the workers ended the strike. According to the Federal Labor Law of 1930, the next step required the appointment by the board of a commission of experts to determine the companies' ability to pay. After an investigation, the three-man commission concluded that the companies were in a position to increase their total labor outlay by 26 million _pesos_ and also recommended that only a limited number of confidential positions should be filled by nonunion men. [39] This last provision was to become most significant, for the companies charged it deprived them of management control. On the recommendation of the commission, the federal board on 28 December 1937 handed down an award in favor of the Petroleum Workers Union; and the oil companies, claiming inability to comply, appealed to the Supreme Court of Mexico. The board's decision was upheld by the court on 1 March 1938. On 14 March the oil companies gave formal notice of their inability to comply with the Supreme Court's ruling. The Federal Conciliation and Arbitration Board then officially terminated, at the request of the union, the contract between the oil companies and the workers. Thus a complete work stoppage was imminent, and this crisis furnished the official justification for the expropriation decree issued by President Cardenas on 18 March 1938.

Just what transpired during the critical period of 1–18 March is a matter of conjecture for those who were not present. Some observers held that the foreign oil companies were willing to pay the total amount of the award provided control of management remain with them. [40] According to President Cardenas, no such offer was made until after the expropriation was announced over the radio on 18 March. [41]

In an address given on the date of the promulgation of the expropriation decree, the Mexican president claimed that the foreign oil companies had refused to obey the mandate of the Supreme Court. The expropriatory action, he noted, involved not simply the execution of the court's judgment by means of attachment of their properties, but involved the "very sovereignty of the nation. . . ."[42] He excoriated the foreign-controlled companies for allegedly failing to provide social investments (such as schools, hospitals, electricity, and so forth) for the oil workers and their families, for maintaining independent police forces, and for discrimination against Mexican workers with regard to wages and working conditions.[43] Countering President Cardenas' charges, Standard Oil Company (N. J.), claimed that the oil companies brought prosperity to Mexico in direct proportion to the readiness of the Mexican government to permit the companies to operate efficiently. Instead of "exploiting" the Mexican people, Standard Oil maintained, the oil industry paid the highest wages in Mexico. They spent more than $1.25 billion in Mexico in the form of taxes, purchases, wages, and contributions of all kinds, which helped materially to raise standards of living in Mexico.[44] In a lively passage in its white paper, the company further charged,

> As soon as it became apparent that the Americans had struck oil in a big way, the incredulity of the Mexican politicians gave way to envy, and indifference was transmuted into cupidity. The temptation to appropriate what foreign ingenuity, energy, and capital were developing in Mexico proved irresistable. Slowly but surely the Mexican Government reached out its fingers and began to squeeze.[45]

The Mexican Supreme Court on 2 December 1939 affirmed the legality of the expropriation decree. Although upholding the companies' right to compensation, the court held that no indemnity was to be paid for the oil in the ground.

Failing to receive immediate compensation for their expropriated properties, the foreign-owned oil companies reacted by bringing pressure to boycott Mexican petroleum in world markets. For example, they threatened to refuse to deal with shipping companies transporting Mexican oil; and they pressured producers of equipment for petroleum production and refining to refuse to sell to Mexico.[46] Thus, Mexico lost its traditional overseas markets. The Anglo-American boycott, accentuated by a business slump in the United States, resulted in a severe drop in Mexican oil exports. From 2.5 million barrels exported in February 1938, outward shipments plunged to 300,000 barrels in April, one month after expropriation.[47] Exports of petroleum fell off nearly 60 percent from 1937-38.[48] The resultant loss in Mexico's foreign exchange earnings forced Mexico to devalue the peso from 3.60 to the dollar to about five to the dollar.

These circumstances placed Mexico in a dilemma. The government was forced through economic necessity to conclude trade agreements with Germany and Italy for the disposal of Mexico's oil, while at the same time it was helping the Loyalists in the Spanish Civil War. Thus economic necessity forced Mexico to compromise her political ideology. Mexican oil exports again reached two million barrels in July 1939, due almost solely to German purchases. [49] However, with the outbreak of World War II, Mexico's petroleum exports went almost exclusively to the United States.

Following great controversy over the values to be assigned to the expropriated properties, agreements were concluded with the American companies between 1940 and 1942 and, after prolonged negotiations, with the British and Dutch interests in 1947. The first claim settlement, reached on 1 May 1940 between the government of President Cardenas and the Sinclair Oil group, acting independently, provided for the payment of $7.5 million (see Table 3.4). Two years later, on 18 April 1942, a joint U.S.-Mexican commission reached an agreement providing for the payment of about $24 million to Standard Oil (N.J.) and the other American interests. This sum was to be paid by the Mexican government to the U.S. government on behalf of the expropriated American companies. A supplementary agreement was arrived at in September 1943, providing for additional compensation of $5,141,709, representing interest at three percent on all unpaid balances from the date of expropriation to 30 September 1947. [50] Finally, on 2 September 1947, President Miguel Aleman announced settlement of claims of the Royal-Dutch Shell group with respect to the "El Aguila" properties for about $82 million plus an additional $49 million in interest from March 1938 to the date of the debt's maturity.

As Table 3.4 indicates, the agreed amounts regarding compensation were far below what the foreign oil companies claimed. The companies placed a value as high as $450 million (U.S. investors, $200 million; Royal-Dutch Shell, $250 million) on their surface installations, other tangible assets, and the oil underground. The value of indemnification on principal, on the other hand, totaled only $113 million (American companies, $31.5 million; Royal-Dutch Shell, $81.7 million). Thus, the ratio of the total value claimed to the value of actual compensation was on the order of four to one (six to one for the U.S. companies; three to one for the Royal-Dutch Shell group).

A major factor accounting for the valuation differences was Mexico's insistence that the companies' claims against oil reserves were invalid, since these deposits remained in the subsurface and were therefore constitutionally inalienable from the national patrimony. [51] The following estimates throw some light on the valuation controversy. According to Moody's Governments and Municipals, Mexico's petroleum industry in 1928 was capitalized at $780 million— wells, tanks, pipelines, and equipment, $544 million; and oil-producing lands, $236 million. [52] In that year, 97 percent of the industry's ownership was in foreign hands. It should be noted that the value of the oil-producing lands (that is, the petroleum in the ground) was

TABLE 3.4

Compensation Claimed and Received by the Foreign–Controlled
Petroleum Companies in Mexico

Companies	Claimed by Foreign Companies	Compensation Received on Principal
Sinclair Oil Group	–	$ 7,500,000
Standard Oil Co. (N.J.) and other companies	–	23,995,991
		31,495,991
U.S. companies total	$200,000,000	
Royal–Dutch Shell Group	250,000,000	81,745,991
Grand total	450,000,000	112,745,991

Sources: For amounts claimed by companies, see J. Lloyd Meecham, A Survey of United States–Latin American Relations (Boston: Houghton Mifflin Co., 1965), p. 369. For actual compensation on the agreed principal, see J. Richard Powell, The Mexican Petroleum Industry: 1938–1950 (Berkeley and Los Angeles: University of California Press, 1956), pp. 158–60.

capitalized at 30 percent of total investment. Another estimate, including the value of oil-producing lands, indicates that the foreign oil companies had a stake in Mexico of $382 million in 1935 (see Table 3.3). The Brookings Institution, as mentioned in the previous section, placed the value of U.S. petroleum properties, including oil lands, at $206 million for 1935, on the eve of their expropriation. It would appear, then, that the capitalized value of the oil underground (which was under contention) provides only a partial explanation for the disparity in oil property valuations.

EVALUATION OF MEXICAN POLICIES

An evaluation of Mexican policies towards foreign investment can only be rendered in the context of Mexico's ambivalent goals since the 1910 revolution: economic independence and development. Beginning with the expropriation of foreign-owned properties by President Lazaro Cardenas in the latter 1930s, the nation has achieved notable success in "the reconquest of Mexico for the Mexicans." In the mid-1930s, foreign interests in Mexico controlled 95 percent of the nation's oil production and refining, 95 percent of mining production, 79 percent of the railways and street cars, and 100 percent of both electric power and telephone service.[53] As Table 3.2 indicates, control over these industries passed by various means—expropriation, nationalization, or "Mexicanization"—into Mexican public or private hands.

The goal of "economic independence," however, has been purchased at a cost to the Mexican economy. For instance, high production and export taxes on mines[54] and changing interpretations of the "Mexicanization" policy inhibited foreign participation in expanding the production of lead, zinc, copper, gold, and silver— despite the fact that these are commodities in which Mexico has traditionally enjoyed a comparative advantage in world markets. The mining industry long has been declining in relation to other sectors of Mexico's expanding economy. In the years 1929 and 1943, mining represented 10 percent of the nation's GNP, but by 1950 it had declined to 3 percent and in 1972 to less than 1.5 percent. Except for iron ore mining, in which the Mexican government assumed a key role, and the special temporary case of sulphur extraction, Mexico has performed poorly in the development of its mining sector compared with most other mineralrich nations in Latin America (see Table 3.5). Between 1947-48 and 1969-70, for example, Mexico's production of lead and silver declined, copper production stagnated, and the output of zinc increased very slowly. In both Peru and Chile, in sharp contrast to Bolivia and Mexico, foreign investment and output responded positively to mining legislation designed to stimulate the growth and diversification of exports.

TABLE 3.5

Mining Production in Selected Latin American Countries,
1947–48 and 1969–70
(thousands of metric tons)*

	Bolivia	Chile	Mexico	Peru
Copper				
Average 1947–48	7	447	63	21
Average 1969–70	8	692	64	210
Iron ore				
Average 1947–48	—	2,280	368	—
Average 1969–70	3	11,399	3,925	9,491
Lead				
Average 1947–48	—	—	214	51
Average 1969–70	25	1	174	156
Silver				
Average 1947–48	6,898	—	58,182	10,036
Average 1969–70	6,414	2,984	42,870	37,861
Sulphur				
Average 1947–48	—	—	3	—
Average 1969–70	26	47	1,489	—
Tin				
Average 1947–48	39	—	—	—
Average 1969–70	29	—	—	23
Zinc				
Average 1947–48	—	—	192	59
Average 1969–70	36	1	260	300

*Except for silver, which is stated in ounces.

Sources: U.S. Department of the Interior, Bureau of Mines, Mineral Yearbook, 1947, 1948 and selected reprints from Mineral Yearbook 1970 (Washington, D.C.: Government Printing Office).

The disinclination of Mexican policymakers to reach an accommodation with foreign investors in the mineral industries, in which large scale venture capital and advanced technology are often decisive factors, suggests that the nation has foregone an opportunity for greater regional dispersion of production and employment. Among the several economic activities of a nation, mining and petroleum exploration offer the best opportunity for opening remote, stagnant regions. (The fortuitous distribution of mineral deposits in most cases bears no relationship to spatial patterns of market-oriented industry and commerce). The development of large scale mines and oil wells in these least accessible regions can provide, in addition to well-paying jobs for workers in the vicinity, new tax bases for both provincial and central governments and a new source of foreign exchange.

Mexico's decision in 1938 to reserve petroleum development exclusively for a state enterprise, Petroleos Mexicanos (PEMEX), also may have had its economic cost. Prior to this decision, Mexico had in 1921 attained the position of the second most important oil-producing nation, with output reaching the historic peak of 193 million barrels, or nearly one-fourth of the world's oil. PEMEX, notwithstanding its massive investment program and recent improvements in organization, has yet to equal that figure.

In Mexico the sovereignty versus development dilemma is particularly evident in the context of the role of multinational firms in Latin American regional economic integration. For example, economies of scale leading to significant cost reductions would be obtainable in both the automotive and petrochemical industries through regional market integration. However, the push for regional integration is opposed generally by Latin American governments if it becomes a means for the spread of foreign enterprise and outside domination of key sectors of the national economies. This attitude has in fact become a major obstacle to the progress of the Latin American Free Trade Association (LAFTA). Mexican government officials have been quoted to the effect that "no nation in Latin America should serve as a launching pad for invasions of other LAFTA members by foreign-controlled firms."[55]

Jack Behrman in his study The Role of International Companies in Latin American Integration notes that Latin American nations predisposed to public ownership of the petrochemicals industry face a choice between maintenance of such state enterprises and the capacity to compete internationally. In Mexico, as we have noted, development of the basic petrochemical industry is reserved for PEMEX, a state enterprise. Multinational companies, however, are reluctant to release their advanced technology—especially the latest designs or processes—except to affiliates that are at least majority held by the parent firm.[56] As a consequence, it is doubtful that Mexico's PEMEX could compete against foreign-controlled petrochemicals enterprises in Brazil and Argentina within an integrated regional market for petrochemical products or could lower its costs sufficiently to enable it to penetrate extraregional (world) markets.

The new "dependence theorists" of Mexico and other Latin American nations contend that import substitution industrialization based on the enterprise of multinational corporations had produced harmful effects for their societies. They hold such enterprisess responsible for engaging in the production of commodities unwarranted by domestic market conditions, involving the use of inappropriate capital intensive technologies that cause unemployment and social "marginalization," and for the erosion of the national entrepreneur class.

It seems fair to ask, however, whether the fault lies with the multinational companies or with the Latin American governments that designed the industrialization policies to which those companies have responded. For example, had these governments taken the Latin American Free Trade Association seriously and shaped their development policies accordingly, foreign-owned enterprises operating within their national markets would no doubt be far more efficient (and their technologies more appropriate) than those currently operating there. One might ask further whether social "marginalization" and the associated high levels of unemployment justifiably can be blamed on foreign investment rather than on rampant population growth in Mexico and other Latin American countries.

The "Mexicanization" policy, though according majority ownership and control to native entrepreneurs, may inhibit national economic development. Whenever domestic savings are used to purchase a controlling share of a foreign-owned affiliate, there is no necessary expansion of the nation's industrial plant or of the number of jobs. The substitution of native management for foreign management following induced "Mexicanization" may lower the efficiency level of the joint enterprise. Finally, the nation's pattern of income distribution may be affected adversely (that is, become even more concentrated) because only the most wealthy Mexican business groups have financial and managerial resources to associate with foreign-controlled, large scale mining and manufacturing enterprises. In short, "Mexicanization" may lead to concentration of profits in fewer hands, higher costs and prices, and a lower level of capital formation.

In vacillating between the extremes of "Cardenismo" and "Alemanismo," Mexican foreign investment policies since 1917 have responded to the twin pulls of revolutionary ideology and the quest for development. Among Latin American nations, Mexico has been singularly successful in achieving both greater national autonomy and, since 1940, rapid and sustained economic development.

NOTES

1. "Stabilizing Development: A Decade of Economic Strategy in Mexico," presented at the annual meeting of the IBRD and the IMF, September 1969, Washington, D.C. Reproduced in El Mercado de Valores Supplement 29, no. 44, (3 November 1969): 11.

2. Howard Cline, Mexico: Revolution to Evolution 1940-1960 (New York: Oxford University Press, 1963), p. 20.

3. The Mexican Yearbook, 1920-21 (Los Angeles: Mexican Yearbook Publishing Co., 1922), pp. 167-69.

4. Raymond Vernon, The Dilemma of Mexico's Development (Cambridge: Harvard University Press, 1963), p. 44.

5. Mira Wilkins, The Emergence of Multinational Enterprise (Cambridge, Mass.: Harvard University Press, 1970), p. 118.

6. Nacional Financiera, S.A., Statistics on the Mexican Economy (Mexico, D.F.: Nacional Financiera, S.A., 1966), p. 25, table 4.

7. "La Politica Mexicana de Fomento Industrial," El Mercado de Valores 28, no. 41 (7 October 1968).

8. "Asamblea Anual de CONCAMIN," El Mercado de Valores 27, no. 15 (10 April 1967): 315-16.

9. Herbert K. May and Jose Antonio Fernandez Arena, Impact on Foreign Investment in Mexico (Washington, D.C.: National Chamber Foundation; and New York: Council of the Americas, 1972), p. 29.

10. "Direct Foreign Investment in Mexico," Comercio Exterior de Mexico 17, no. 12 (December 1971): 10-11.

11. May and Arena, op. cit., p. 82, table 32.

12. U.S. Direct Investments Abroad, Part II: Investment Position, Financial and Operating Data, U.S. Department of Commerce, BEA-Sup 72-01, 1972, p. 65, table 14.

13. Lacy H. Hunt, II, "Industrial Development on the Mexican Border," Business Review, Federal Reserve Bank of Dallas (February 1970): 4.

14. Dilmus D. James and John S. Evans, "The Industrialization of the Northern Mexican Border Region: Past, Present, and Future" (unpublished manuscript), p. 13, table I.

15. Richard Bolin, "Border Industry Facts for 1973," Mexican-American Review 41, no. 9 (September 1973): 14.

16. May and Arena, op. cit., p. 30.

17. New York Times, 15 October 1937, p. 5.

18. Harry K. Wright, Foreign Enterprise in Mexico (Chapel Hill: University of North Carolina Press, 1971), p. 151.

19. Brookings Institution data cited by Edgar Turlington, "Foreign Investments in Mexico," Annals of the American Academy 208 (March 1940): 105.

20. Wright, op. cit., p. 71.

21. Moody's Railroads: American and Foreign (New York: Moody's Investors, Inc., 1949), p. 1387.

22. Information received by the author from the Bank of Mexico, Department of Economic Studies.

23. Cline, op. cit., p. 284.

24. See R. G. Hawkins, et al., Stabilization of Export Receipts and Economic Development, (New York: New York University Press, 1966), pp. 111-12.

25. Joseph Grunwald and Philip Musgrove, Natural Resources in Latin American Development, published for Resources for the Future, Inc. (Baltimore: Johns Hopkins Press, 1970), p. 166.

26. "Anaconda Company 1973 Annual Report," p. 9.

27. Ifigenia M. de Navarette, Los Incentivos Fiscales y el Desarrollo Economico de Mexico (Mexico City: Universidad Nacional Autonoma de Mexico, 1967), p. 77.

28. Secretaria de Governacion, Law to Promote Mexican Investment and to Regulate Foreign Investment (Mexico, D. F.: Government of Mexico, 1973), p. 8.

29. Ibid., p. 7.

30. For an excellent discussion of Echeverria's policies, see Edward H. Moseley, "New Direction for the Mexican Revolution, 1970-1974," Delphian Quarterly 57, no. 2 (Spring 1974): 10-18.

31. U. S., Congress, House, Committee on Interstate and Foreign Commerce, Fuel Investigation: Mexican Petroleum, 80th Cong., 2nd sess., 1949, p. 116 (hereinafter cited as Fuel Investigation).

32. Ibid., p. 117.

33. Fredda Jean Bullard, Mexico's Natural Gas (Austin: University of Texas Bureau of Business Research, 1968), p. 4.

34. Fuel Investigation, op. cit., p. 118.

35. J. Lloyd Mecham, A Survey of United States-Latin American Relations (Boston: Houghton Mifflin, 1965), p. 364.

36. Ibid., p. 366.

37. Ibid.

38. U. S. Tariff Commission, Commercial Policies and Trade Relations: Mexico (Washington, D. C.: Government Printing Office, 1940), p. 24.

39. Government of Mexico, Mexico's Oil (Mexico, D. F.: Government of Mexico, 1940), p. xliii.

40. Wendel C. Gordon, The Expropriation of Foreign-Owned Property in Mexico (Washington, D. C.: American Council on Public Affairs, 1941), p. 109.

41. Ibid., p. 117.

42. Fuel Investigation, op. cit., p. 121.

43. Ibid., p. 122.

44. Standard Oil Co. (N. J.), "Confiscation or Expropriation? Mexico's Seizure of the Foreign Owned Oil Industry," no date,
p. 93.

45. Ibid., p. 11.

46. John S. Evans, "The Evolution of the Mexican Tax System, with Special Reference to Developments Since 1956, unpublished Ph.D. dissertation, University of Wisconsin, 1971, p. 78.

47. Maurice Halperin, "Mexico Shifts Her Foreign Policy,"
Foreign Affairs 17, no. 4 (October 1940): 207.

48. Fuel Investigation, op. cit., p. 8.

49. William O. Scroggs, "Mexican Oil and World Politics,"
Foreign Affairs 17, no. 3 (1940): 172-74.

50. Moody's Governments and Municipals (New York:
Moody's Investors, Inc., 1950), pp. 1888-89.

51. Bullard, op. cit., p. 8.

52. Moody's Governments and Municipals: American and
Foreign (New York: Moody's Investors, Inc., 1929), pp. 749-50.

53. Alfredo Navarrette, "La Inversion Extranjera Directa
en Mexico," El Mercado de Valores 26, no. 44 (October 1966):
1080; and U.S. Tariff Commission, Agricultural, Pastoral and Forest
Industries in Mexico (Washington, D.C.: Government Printing Office,
1946), pp. 23-4.

54. Evans, op. cit., pp. 21-4.

55. D.M. Kiefer, "Mexico Strives for Industrial Independence," Chemical and Engineering News 11, no. 12 (4 December
1967): 99

56. Jack N. Behrman, The Role of International Companies
in Latin American Integration, published for the Committee for Economic Development (Lexington, Mass.: D.C. Heath, 1972), p. 66.

4

U.S. MINERAL INVESTMENTS AND CHILEAN NATIONALISM: PROBLEMS OF AN "ENCLAVE" INDUSTRY

A mine is not a thing lying about to be taken. A mine is created—an ore deposit is a pile of rock under capital, management, labor, science and technology, cooperative environment, demand and market focus to make it a mine. Not until then is it an asset to a government or to a company.
—President of the Anaconda Company, cited in Simon G. Hanson, Dollar Diplomacy Modern Style (Washington, D. C.: Inter-American Press, 1970), p. 59.

In Chile, as in several other Latin American nations, romantic nationalism has vied with the more pragmatic variety to shape the policies, terms, and conditions, under which U. S. companies have been permitted to extract, process, and export mineral resources. The so-called "Chileanization" policy initiated during President Eduardo Frei's term of office (October 1964 to October 1970) produced an accommodation that appeared to satisfy both the aspirations of Chilean nationalists and the basic conditions of the U. S. copper mining companies. Indeed, the "Chileanization" or partnership approach was acclaimed widely as the viable organizational formula for attracting U. S. mineral investments to Latin America.

This chapter examines the Gran Mineria's postwar responses to the frequently changing investment climate in Chile, that is, the policy of onerous taxation, the "New Deal" Law, the "Chileanization" agreements, and negotiated nationalization.

The author draws heavily on data compiled by the Central Bank of Chile and on reports issued by Chilean Copper Corporation (CODELCO), the Chilean Development Corporation (CORFO), the

International Monetary Fund (IMF), and the U.S. copper mining firms. He also benefited from discussions with Chilean economists, businessmen, and engineers during his Fulbright Fellowship year in Chile in 1957.

The period under investigation extends from 1944, when Chile captured one-fifth of the world copper market, to 1970, the year that Senator Salvador Allende, the leader of the Marxist ruling coalition, Unidad Popular, was confirmed as president by the Chilean Congress.

STRUCTURE AND ORGANIZATION OF CHILE'S COPPER MINING INDUSTRY

An outstanding feature of Chile's economy since the mid-1920s has been its considerable dependence on the export of a single primary commodity—copper. Moreover, until the latter 1960s, the affiliates of two U.S.-owned firms—the Anaconda Company and the Kennecott Copper Corporation—dominated Chile's copper mining industry, a fact that from time to time posed conflict between the nation's longrange economic opportunities and more immediate political realities.[1]

Although Anaconda's Chilean operations took place in so-called "export enclaves," the U.S. companies exercised a powerful impact on the Chilean economy by virtue of their sizeable tax payments, purchases from local suppliers, and outlays for wages, salaries, and fringe benefits. Anaconda's Chilean properties were located at different sites in the Atacama Desert far to the north. The most important of these, Chuquicamata, the world's largest open-pit mine, lies at an elevation of 9,000 feet. The complex includes concentrating, smelting, and refining facilities and formerly company-owned power and water facilities. Kennecott's single Chilean subsidiary, the Braden Copper Company, operated El Teniente, the world's largest underground copper mine, a processing plant, a railroad, housing, schools, and other facilities in the mountains southeast of Santiago at an elevation of 7,000 feet above sea level.

"Big Mining" (known locally as the Gran Mineria) refers to those companies that are highly mechanized and annually produce at least 75,000 metric tons of smelted or refined copper.[2] During the 1960s, the Gran Mineria produced from 85 to 90 percent of Chile's copper. In 1970, the physical operations of the Gran Mineria took place in three mining sites involving the application of a high degree of mechanization and technical and organizational expertise. Large scale output permitted extraordinary efficiency, enabling the U.S. companies to produce at low unit costs. The source of Anaconda's and Kennecott's contribution to Chile's economy was the enormous

64

productivity of the U. S.-controlled firms. In the period 1950-54, for example, average productivity in the Gran Mineria was

> . . . eleven times greater than that of the economy as a whole, about thirteen times that of industry and almost twenty times that of agriculture. In these great disparities lies the fundamental reason why copper plays such an important role in the Chilean economy. [3]

The development of a large copper mine and its related facilities normally involves a minimum investment of $100 million. It takes from four to six years to develop a new copper mine or to substantially increase the capacity of an existing one. The large Chilean orebodies are massive, containing 100 million tons or more of ore of highly uniform grade, of between 1 and 2 percent copper content.

The discovery of the Tamaya mines in 1833 marked the beginning of an upward trend that culminated in Chile's becoming the largest producer of copper in the world in 1851. Chile's maximum production during the 19th century was reached in 1876, when 38 percent of the world's copper production reportedly came from that nation's mines. [4] Thereafter, the Chilean share in world copper output dropped rapidly from 14.6 percent during 1881-90 to 5.7 percent during 1891-1900. [5]

Chile's initial preeminence in global copper production was based on the existence of extremely rich surface ores (assaying between 20 and 50 percent copper) that could be worked by primitive methods. The eventual exhaustion of these rich ores called for a new type of entrepreneur, one would could apply the technology of large scale production for working lower grade ores and mobilize the associated risk capital. As Joseph Grunwald and Philip Musgrove observed, the development of the lower grade orebodies "required investments much larger than those that had previously attracted local capital. Chilean investors were unable or unwilling to finance those projects; as a result, foreign enterprises came to dominate the industry." [6]

Coexisting with the Gran Mineria is the medium and small group of mines disposing of more rudimentary production techniques. Structurally, the group's operations comprise 11 medium-sized plants and several thousands of small mining operators primarily using hand tools. The medium-sized firms were variously owned by Chilean, French, Canadian, and U.S. capital. Referring to the status of the national firms in the 1950s, the Chilean geographer Pedro Cunil Grau noted that "it is evident that our economic and technical resources do not under present conditions permit a radical quantitative transformation so necessary in the mining industry. . . . "[7] The medium and small group has been subsidized heavily by the government, indirectly through the foreign exchange system (up to 1955) and directly through the provision of low interest loans. Tax rates are also much lower than those affecting the Gran Mineria. Chile's private enterprise, in the view of Tom Sanders, "lacks both the tradition and the technical capacity to work in copper production. Its investing instincts are so timid that the government must use cajolery and guarantee a substantial profit in the undertaking of new ventures. "[8]

THE INTERNATIONAL COPPER ECONOMY AND
POLICY CONSTRAINTS IN CHILE

Although deposits of copper are to be found in all of the major world geographic regions, the mining of copper is concentrated in a few countries, reflecting the unequal and fortuitous distribution of world copper reserves. Following the United States, the most important mine producers of copper are the USSR, Chile, Zambia (formerly Northern Rhodesia), Canada, and Zaire (formerly the Congo). Until the latter 1960s, a handful of large companies—three American, two British, and one Belgian—jointly disposed of about 60 percent of the non-Communist world's production.[9] The largest copper mining companies are vertically integrated, either owning or controlling smelters and refineries, and some even control copper fabricating enterprises.[10]

The principal markets for copper are found in the highly industrialized countries, that is, the United States, Western Europe, and Japan. The red metal is used mainly by such important industries as construction, transportation, and machinery and equipment, and in electrical and electronic products. Thus, it is commonplace for the price of copper to fluctuate widely with business cycles generated in these leading industrialized nations.

In addition to the non-Communist world copper mining capacity, estimated at 5.7 million metric tons in 1969, other elements enter into the determination of the short-run supply: the stocks producers and fabricators have on hand, the possibility of recovering copper from scrap, and the existence of strategic stockpiles held by governments. Hence, during the periods of extreme shortage, primary copper can be released from inventories and stockpiles to dampen the price of copper and to meet consumer requirements at more stable prices.

Although the world copper market fits the general description of a standardized oligopoly—the lion's share being supplied by a few firms[11]—the red metal nevertheless faces price competition from alternate materials—aluminum, plastics, and the newer alloyed steels—has occurred, both in the United States and in Western Europe. [12] Most of the markets for copper products that have been lost to other materials are not recovered easily. The danger of substitution induced the major companies to adjust their production and investment plans accordingly. "Our object," according to Sir Robert Prain, retired chairman of Zambia's formerly U.S.-controlled Roan Selection Trust, "has always been the maintenance of reasonable and stable prices." [13]

A series of conferences involving representatives of the major copper exporting nations resulted in the creation during 1967 of the Inter-Governmental Council of Copper Exporting Countries (CIPEC). Conceivably, the CIPEC countries (Chile, Peru, Zaire, and Zambia), which together in 1970 accounted for over 40 percent of free world copper mining capacity and 53 percent of world copper exports, have the ability to exercise considerable leverage over copper prices while, as during the early 1970s, the metal remains in short supply. By 1970 Chile, Zambia, and Zaire already had acquired majority ownership in the large copper properties, and Peru intervened as marketing agent. It is doubtful, however, whether these nations can muster the necessary discipline and financial resources during periods of market balance or surplus to agree on and enforce a high price policy. With the determination of the Indo-China War and the anticipated rapid expansion of world copper mining capacity, surpluses of copper are being forecast for the latter 1970s. Because of the xenophobic nationalism associated with their mineral policies, it is unlikely that the CIPEC countries will continue to attract the venture capital from abroad required to maintain their share of the world market.

Until the mid-1960s, the framework of the international copper economy and Chile's underdeveloped status appreciably limited that nation's freedom of action in relation to the U.S. companies. Chilean copper policy had to maneuver within a set of constraints during most of the postwar period. The three principal constraints were (1) Chile's copper deposits could be developed on a large scale and an efficient basis only by large foreign-controlled companies; (2) the U.S. companies presumably contemplated a range of investment alternatives that geographically encompassed the hemisphere and normally weighed risks (including political uncertainty) against the expected rate of return after taxes; and (3) Chile's limited postwar share in world copper mining output precluded the possibility (except during a severe market imbalance) of unilaterally fixing the market price of copper to her own benefit.

Because of both a high initial risk and a long gestation period in developing a mine, a foreign investor must expect a high rate of return if he is to commit his venture capital. Typically, multinational mining enterprises expect to generate an internal rate of return on their investment of around 15 percent. Assuming a three-year development phase during which the mine is not productive, with capital expenditures spread evenly over three years, "to yield a 15 percent internal rate of return over the 10-year period, annual after-tax profits as a percentage of capital expenditures would need to average about 23 percent. "[14]

In an effort to improve unilaterally the nation's terms of trade with the rest of the world, the Chilean government in 1953-54 attempted an operation that has been described aptly as "monopoly on a shoe-string. "[15] After gaining control over the price of copper in Chile, the nation's Central Bank set the price unilaterally at 36.5 cents per pound between early 1952 and October 1953. However, because there was an adequate world supply of copper at lower prices, supply exceeded demand at the Central Bank's price. Chile's copper exports were hampered and unsold stocks accumulated as the months went by. Notwithstanding the fall in mining production, 110,000 tons of copper remained unsold at the end of 1953. Finally, the U.S. government agreed to buy 100,000 tons of the metal at the old price of 30 cents per pound for its strategic stockpile. The Chilean government overestimated the degree of market power it could wield in world copper markets. *

Other considerations also should be kept in mind. Even if Chile had temporarily succeeded in its price-rigging operation, the United States and England—through release of vast supplies of copper from their strategic reserves into world markets—at any time could have neutralized such action. Furthermore, a unilateral intervention such as attempted by Chile, even if successful in the short-run, risks the dangerous long-run prospect of competing countries expanding their capacities to produce the metal. Brazil, whose international market power in coffee is still considerable, has faced similar difficulties.

---

*With only one-eighth of world production and an assumed price elasticity of demand of unity for the world copper industry, a 24 percent output cutback (assuming no release of stocks into the market) will decrease world supply by only 3 percent and increase price by 3 percent. Assuming an initial price of 33 cents per pound of copper, Chile's unilateral output reduction would increase the price by only one cent a pound. During periods of extreme copper shortage, marked by an excess of demand over supply and rationing by copper producers, characterized by the years 1966-70, the Chilean government could force a price rise in segments of the world market. See "Report on Copper," World Business, The Chase Manhattan Bank (15 April 1969): 10-12.

THE POLICY OF ONEROUS TAXATION, 1946-54

Notwithstanding an extremely favorable world copper market from 1946-54, the Gran Mineria suffered protracted contraction of its operations under the pressure of increased taxes, foreign exchange penalties, and official control of copper sales. According to one local authority,

> The Chilean copper industry was marching rapidly toward its own destruction and it was clearly indicated that in the not too distant future, the country would face a general economic crisis resulting from the drastic reduction in foreign exchange income. [16]

The Chilean treasury could capture an ever-growing share of the Gran Mineria's income—but only at the cost of repelling new foreign investment in copper mining and consequent erosion of the future tax base. Given this short-sighted political orientation and the country's limited market power in the international copper economy, Chile lost excellent opportunities in the latter 1940s and early 1950s to attract massive foreign direct investments in its key export sector. [17] Instead, heavy taxes, including foreign exchange penalties, and other inhibiting measures induced the U. S. copper companies (which operated on a hemispheric scale) to abandon expansion plans in Chile and direct capital funds to less productive mineral sites in other countries offering a more favorable investment climate. The sharp rise in prices paid for copper during the immediate postwar decade (from 11.7 cents per pound in 1945 to 29.9 cents in 1954) was not allowed to serve as a stimulant to production and investment in the Chilean industry because of the "returned value" exchange penalty rate and the "overprice tax" by which Chile's treasury systematically appropriated these increments.

By the early 1950s, taxes (including hidden taxes) levied on the U. S.-owned copper companies in Chile exceeded 80 percent of net profits, [18] while the total tax rate on copper mining in 1952 was below 50 percent for all of the other important producing countries, and for several it was 30 percent or less. [19] Chilean taxation of the U. S.-owned companies in 1952, included the following: (1) an income tax of 60 percent levied on the difference between the sales price in New York and the cost of copper delivered to that market; (2) customs duties; (3) a special "overprice tax" on sales, established in May 1952, which authorized the government to retain the proceeds of sales over and above a price of 24.5 cents per pound; and (4) an implicit or hidden tax on the local costs of production.

The Gran Mineria's obligation to surrender copper dollars to the government at a fixed, overvalued (penalty) rate of exchange carried with it an implicit tax on the domestic cost of production whose yield continued to rise with the advance of inflation. Essentially, it penalized the companies' use of Chilean labor. Considering the more realistic exchange rate of 115 pesos per dollar for 1952, as determined by the purchasing power parity formula, the application of the 19.37 pesos per dollar penalty rate converted Chile from one of the lowest cost copper mining countries (in U.S. dollars) to one of the highest in the world.[20] For example, labor costs per pound of copper at Kennecott's El Teniente mine rose sharply from 3.7 cents in 1945 to 12.5 cents in 1954. With the elimination of the penalty exchange rate in 1955, the unit cost fell back to 4.1 cents.[21]

The Gran Mineria's response to these official measures was a severe contraction in output and associated copper export sales, and a postponement of capital outlays in Chilean copper mining during 1950-54 with increased investment in marginal mines in the United States.[22] The statistics on U.S. investments in Chilean mining and smelting, which included construction of a sulfide ore treatment plant at Chuquicamata at a cost of $130 million[23] obscured the fact that net disinvestment in copper mining occurred during 1950-54.

The Gran Mineria's share in world mine production of copper shrank from 19 percent in the latter phase of World War II (1943-45) to a postwar nadir of 11.6 percent in 1953-54. Chile, which had long held second place (next to the United States) in world copper production, was dislodged in 1953 by Rhodesia (now Zambia) for that position. In absolute terms, the Gran Mineria's copper output fell from 467,000 metric tons on average during 1943-45 to an average 324,000 tons (see Table 4.1) during 1953-54—a drop of 31 percent. Finally, the companies were forced to respond to the penalty rate of exchange (an implicit tax on the use of Chilean labor) by cutting back on the labor force, with the result that from 1945-54 employment in the Gran Mineria declined by more than one-third, from 17,385 to 11,057. The rapidly rising prices paid for copper in the immediate postwar decade (from 11.7 cents per pound in 1945 to 29.9 cents in 1954) were not allowed to act as a stimulant to production and expansion in the Chilean industry because of the "returned value" penalty rate and the "overprice tax" by which Chile's treasury systematically appropriated these increments. In effect, there was merely a large transfer of income from the Gran Mineria to other sectors of the economy. While, on the one hand, the government captured a growing share of total sales from the foreign copper companies, these very measures, over a number of years, served to contract the essential base on which the taxes were applied. The policy was inherently self-defeating.

The large surplus that accrued to the Chilean economy during this period from its chief export sector was largely dissipated on current consumption through transfer payments, subsidies, and preferential

TABLE 4.1

The Gran Mineria: Copper Mining Production, Copper Prices,
and Value Returned, 1944-70

		Production		Prices		Total Value Returned*	
Year	(millions of dollars)	Metric tons (thousand)	Index (1947=100)	U. S. Cents Per Pound	Index (1947=100)	Millions of Dollars	Percentage
1944	108.7	489.9	120	11.7	54	83.1	76
1945	105.4	462.1	113	11.7	54	79.1	75
1946	100.5	358.6	88	14.8	69	73.5	73
1947	161.7	408.4	100	21.6	100	120.1	74
1948	195.5	424.9	104	22.3	103	133.6	68
1949	137.1	350.7	86	19.4	90	104.4	76
1950	152.0	345.5	85	21.5	100	104.8	69
1951	175.0	360.1	88	26.3	121	127.9	73
1952	249.0	373.8	92	31.7	147	209.2	84
1953	182.0	325.5	80	30.8	143	161.9	89
1954	185.3	323.2	79	29.9	138	143.5	77
1955	310.2	391.7	96	39.1	181	226.7	73
1956	327.7	443.0	109	40.4	187	228.6	70
1957	247.3	434.1	106	27.2	126	191.7	76
1958	199.1	418.7	103	24.1	112	153.4	77
1959	300.5	497.1	122	28.9	134	217.1	72
1960	309.8	478.8	117	29.9	138	233.0	75
1961	270.9	480.8	118	27.9	129	209.1	77
1962	300.4	510.2	125	28.5	132	233.9	78
1963	291.2	507.4	124	28.4	131	224.3	77
1964	340.3	527.8	129	31.0	144	253.9	75
1965	415.0	496.0	122	30.1	140	338.0	81
1966	567.0	538.0	131	54.2	251	450.0	80
1967	602.0	537.0	131	48.6	220	490.0	81
1968	615.0	519.0	127	53.3	247	515.0	84
1969	799.0	540.0	132	66.6	308	688.0	86
1970	750.0	535.0	130	64.2	297	629.0	84

*Value of production—(profits + amortization).

Sources: For 1944-64, Banco Central de Chile, Balanza de Pagos de Chile (various issues, 1944-65); and Boletin Mensual (various issues, 1944-65). For 1965-68, IMF, Balance of Payments Yearbook, vol. 21 (Washington, D.C.: International Monetary Fund, July 1970). For 1969-70, IMF, Balance of Payments Yearbook, vol. 23 (Washington, D.C.: International Monetary Fund, July 1972) (preliminary estimates). Prices for 1965-70 are derived from CORFO, Chile Economic Notes 11, no. 33 (1 January 1973).

exchange rates for imports on foodstuffs, newsprint, and other consumer commodities. [24] Markos Mamalakis writes of Chile's failure to channel the nation's copper surplus into capital formation

> Nevertheless, the use of this surplus for maximum economic growth has been prevented by the lack of proper allocation policy and, in particular, by an inappropriate import policy. Thus, no matter how successful the government might be in raising the sector's foreign exchange and/or government revenue contribution, it cannot succeed in promoting growth unless it pursues a correct allocation policy. [25]

THE "NEW DEAL" LAW REVERSED POLICIES AND INVESTOR RESPONSES, 1955-60

The critical situation involving the status of the Gran Mineria was reversed by the passage of the "New Deal" Law in May 1955. Influential elements of Chile's business, scientific, and engineering communities supported this more rational approach to the Gran Mineria. The new legislation, so instrumental in reviving the industry, placed primary emphasis on profit taxes and provided genuine incentive to the expansion of output. The law eliminated the discriminatory exchange rate on the U.S.-owned companies, restored to them the control over sales, and allowed them to receive the full sales price on copper produced.

As a result, production was increased from available capacity and capital expansion programs totaling $200 million were initiated. The new legislation set in motion intensive prospecting operations and these led to the discovery of two major orebodies (El Salvador and Exotica) by Anaconda and of a third deposit (Rio Blanco) by the Cerro Corporation, a newcomer to the Chilean copper mining scene. Significantly, Anaconda's Exotica orebody of more than 150 million tons of ore with recoverable copper content of about 1.4 percent was discovered by geological, geophysical, and geochemical techniques unknown until that discovery. The nation's proven reserves of copper thus were expanded decisively. Anaconda also responded by investing $118 million to develop the deposit at El Salvador and replace output from the exhausted Potrerillos mine, and $60 million to expand the Chuquicamata open-pit mine. [26]

Output of the Gran Mineria (see Table 4.2), which averaged 324,000 metric tons in 1953-54, the two years preceding the "New Deal" Law, expanded to a yearly average of 488,000 tons in 1959-60, on completion of the investment program—an increase of 50 percent.

Even so, a major critic of the "New Deal" Law, Mario Vera Valenzuela[27] of the University of Chile, maintained that the new government policy did not take full advantage of its copper reserves because
the "nonretained" values were higher than during the five-year period
preceding the law. Valenzuela's argument is irrelevant, since what
is important is the level of "returned values," or Chile's participation in copper sales. In the 1953-54 period, Chile received an average of $153 million or 83 percent of company sales from copper; in
1959-60, on completion of the expansion program, Chile received
and average of $225 million, or 74 percent of sales (see Table 4.1).
Even though the percentage of company sales remaining in Chile
decreased, the income received by the nation rose, and Chile
increased its total copper income by about one-half despite a 1 cent
drop in the average price of copper between 1953-54 and 1959-60.
The anticipated smaller percentage of value remaining in Chile from
each ton of copper exported, resulting from the law's provisions, was
offset by a more than proportional expansion in the physical volume
of shipments abroad.

Finally, it should be remembered that the discriminatory
exchange rate imposed prior to the "New Deal" Law artificially
raised the dollar cost of the Gran Mineria's local purchases, making
it uneconomical for the large copper companies to acquire materials,
supplies, and equipment in Chile. With the elimination of this obstacle, an important market for national industry was created.

NEW TAX MEASURES AND AN OPPORTUNITY FOREGONE, 1961-65

In 1961, the investment climate for the U. S. copper companies again took a turn for the worse: expropriation of their properties became a clear possibility, new copper taxes were imposed, and
company profits again were squeezed. The year before, the U. S.
companies were prepared to launch a second major expansion program in Chile involving an outlay of from $400-500 million. Included
in this outlay was Anaconda's proposal to invest $128 million in an
electrolytic refinery, and Cerro Corporation's offering of $75 mil-
lion to bring its recently discovered Rio Blanco ore deposit, located
southeast of Santiago, into production.

The implementation of the proposed expansion program
depended on Chilean congressional approval of a 20-year tax guarantee, providing continuation of the basic provisions contained in
the "New Deal" Law. In the face of severe political opposition to the
tax guarantee for the U. S. copper companies, the Allesandri administration in 1961 backed down from its intention to introduce the bill

73

in congress. Instead congress levied two surtaxes of five percent and eight percent on top of basic income taxes, despite the agreement in the "New Deal" Law exempting the Gran Mineria from additional taxes. One of the surtaxes was levied to alleviate earthquake damage; the other was imposed to provide pay raises for the army and civil service. Once applied, the additional taxes remained in force and were not repealed until the latter 1960s. These "special taxes" totaling 13 percentage points, raised the tax burden to 79 percent and 84 percent on the net income of Anaconda's Chuquicamata and Kennecott's El Teniente mines, respectively.[28] By contrast, the tax in Zambia, Chile's closest competitor for the second position in world copper production, was less than half this rate.

The Gran Mineria's expansion plans were shelved immediately. Anaconda, for example, decided instead to build a copper refinery in Montana.[29] Cerro Corporation, according to a company spokesman, placed the Rio Blanco project "on the back burner in view of the political and economic situation down there."[30] Kennecott Copper Corporation chose to redirect its capital funds to step up the capacity of its Utah mine—a dramatic example of a less-economic allocation of the world's scarce resources.

> For it means that capital has been diverted into less-productive channels: whereas a ton of Chilean soil yields Kennecott nearly 40 pounds of copper, its Utah deposits are less than half as rich. If producers are forced to rely on poorer grades of ore, the shift inevitably will show up in prices, thereby burdening all consumers of the raw material.[31]

Thus, for a second time in the postwar period, Chile lost an opportunity to increase decisively its foreign exchange earnings capacity. Political attitudes and government policies overruled the technical factors of geology and economics.

Had Chile agreed to a 20-year tax guarantee provision in 1961 (the condition for initiating the second phase of the copper expansion program), the nation would have increased its capacity to produce an additional 390,000 metric tons of copper. By failing to reach an accommodation with the U.S. enterprises at that time, Chile lost, according to my estimates, roughly $1.5 billion of net foreign exchange income between 1966 (when the expansion program would have been completed) and 1972 (the year when President Eduardo Frei's "Chileanization" projects were to be completed.)*

---

*I assume the following: (1) an increase in copper mining capacity of 390,000 metric tons, including activation of La Exotica

"CHILEANIZATION" AND THE INVESTMENT
EXPANSION PROGRAM

A decisive shift in the balance of political power in favor of the Christian Democrats, reflected in the elections of 1964 and 1965, presented Chile with an opportunity to work out a long-range copper agreement. The new policy initiated by President Eduardo Frei enabled the nation to share directly in both ownership and management of the large copper mines. During the months preceding the 1964 presidential elections, both the Christian Democrats (who aspired to power) and the U. S. companies were in a bargaining mood and exploratory talks began. The Christian Democrats were among several political factions that had opposed the Gran Mineria's terms and investment proposals in 1960-61. Four years later, with the prospect of an election victory, they responded favorably to Kennecott's new proposal[32] to bring the government into partnership as a majority stockholder, a formula that would permit dramatic expansion in Chile's copper mining industry. Forsaking the dogmatic appeals of his political rivals on the extreme left, President Frei indicated Chile's logical path toward rapid economic growth.

> I want to remind you that I have always affirmed that the
> basic objective of my policy would be to achieve a sub-
> stantial expansion of the production of copper because it is
> the fundamental instrument of our international trade and
> because it is the only sector where, in a rapid way, we
> would be able to increase our income. [33]

The "Chileanization" program included the following objectives:

(1)   approximately to double Chilean copper output;
(2)   to increase value added in Chile by refining the bulk of
        Chilean copper; and
(3)   to provide for Chilean government participation in the
        production and marketing of copper as a partner of the
        foreign companies.

The $600 million Gran Mineria expansion program (see Table 4. 2) was designed to boost the output of the three existing mines plus two

---

body, which was discovered in 1960; (2) an average copper price of 40 cents per pound; and (3) three-fourths of the value of copper sales remaining in Chile ("retained values"). Given these assumptions, total copper sales would have come to $2, 059 million over the six-year period and Chile's net share to $1, 544, 000.

TABLE 4.2

Gran Mineria: Authorized Investments and Expansion of Mining Capacity Based on "Chileanization" Agreements

	Chilean Government Participation (as of 1 Jan. 1970) (percent)	Authorized Investments	Production Capacity (metric tons)		
			Mid-1960s	1971–72 Projected	Capacity Growth
Anaconda Group					
Andes Copper Mining Co. (El Salvador)	51	$10,304,000	90,000	110,000	20,000
Chile Exploration Co. (Chuquicamata)	51	99,107,000	310,000	390,000	80,000
Cia. Minera Exotica (Exotica)	25	38,000,000	—	112,500	112,500
Housing plan	—	67,500,000	—	—	—
Anaconda total		$214,911,000	400,000	612,500	212,500
Kennecott Coper Copr.					
Soc. Minera El Teniente (El Teniente)	51	$230,241,000	180,000	280,000	100,000
Cerro Corp.					
Cia. Minera Andina (Rio Blanco)	30	$157,000,000	—	77,500	77,500
Total		$602,152,000	580,000	970,000	390,000

Source: CORFO, Economic Notes no. 26 (30 June 1968) and no. 59 (8 May 1970).

new large mines from 580,000 metric tons in the mid-1960s to 970,000 metric tons in 1971-72, thereby significantly raising the South American country's share in the global copper market and, it was anticipated, enabling Chile to become the leading copper exporting nation in the world. Financing of the projects was provided by foreign banks and suppliers ($309 million, including $197 million from the U.S. Export-Import Bank), the U.S. copper companies ($222 million), and most of the remaining from the Chilean Copper Corporation (CODELCO).[34] Significantly, of the $575 million realized investment in the expansion program from 1967-70, $306 million, or 60 percent, was spent within Chile.[35]

The authorized outlays in support of the Anaconda subsidiaries (see Table 4.2) came to $215 million and mining capacity was to be stepped up from 400,000 metric tons in the mid-1960s to 612,000 metric tons by 1971-72. The Anaconda mines accounted for more than third of the authorized investments of the Gran Mineria expansion program and more than one-half of the projected increase in production. Capacity of Kennecott's El Teniente mine was scheduled to grow from 180,000 metric tons to 280,000 metric tons at a cost of $230 million, and Cerro's Rio Blanco deposit was to be brought into production with a capacity of nearly 80,000 metric tons now costing an estimated $157 million.

Kennecott and Cerro had assumed a more flexible posture and retreated from their opposition to state participation in their Chilean operations. On the other hand, they were eager to invest in Chile rather than in higher cost areas; on the other, they faced the probable grim alternative of expropriation in the eventuality of a Christian Democratic defeat.* Through the state-owned Chilean Copper Corporation (CODELCO), the government in 1967 acquired 61 percent of the stock in the reorganization of Kennecott's El Teniente mine and 30 percent of Cerro's Rio Blanco mine. Payments for CODELCO's 51 percent share in El Teniente ($92.7 million) were immediately re-lent to the Chilean government on 15-year terms by their recipient, the Braden Copper Company, Kennecott's subsidiary. After the transfer of the majority of Braden's shares to CODELCO, Kennecott continued to operate the El Teniente mine through a management services contract. Anaconda was reluctant to accept "Chileanization" of its major interests, the Chuquicamata and El Salvador properties. Both Charles M. Brinckerhoff, former chairman of the Anaconda Company, and

---

*In 1964 Senator Salvador Allende (who would subsequently become president in 1970) had a bill in Congress to nationalize the U.S. companies. Under its provisions, they would have received a token $123 million in compensation in the form of bonds paying 3 percent.

C. Jay Parkinson, who succeeded him as chief executive in 1968, refused to sell an interest in the two large mines. Chairman Brinckerhoff spoke fluent Spanish and was a personal friend of President Frei, and Anaconda enjoyed good relations in Chile. "This kept alive the illusion," according to one industry executive, "that Anaconda would always be welcome in Chile."[36] The company did conclude an agreement in 1967 to sell the Chilean government a 25 percent interest in the new Exotica mine and to form a mixed exploration company to be 49 percent Chilean owned. Any new orebodies to be discovered by this enterprise were to be developed jointly. The "Chileanization" agreements were approved officially by the Chilean Congress between December 1966 and March 1967.

Both parties—the Chilean nation and the companies—gained from the terms of the bargain. Chile's copper mining capacity was to be stepped up sharply, thereby increasing national income and foreign exchange earnings; and with the state as a partner in Chile's major export industry, nationalist objections, it was hoped, would be neutralized markedly. The Chilean government through its newly organized Chilean Copper Corporation (CODELCO) achieved a stronger voice in copper operations, including the marketing and pricing of the red metal, and shared directly in the Gran Mineria's profits. The companies in turn received state guarantees against expropriation for all new investments in the industry and secured lower tax rates, along with an agreement providing tax stability over a period of 20 years—conditions that they failed to secure in 1960-61. Moreover, the periodic burden of labor negotiations now would be shared with the Chilean government; and "Chileanization" of the Gran Mineria was to give the U. S. companies a measure of "protective coloration" against ill-informed criticism.

Chile signed an investment guarantee treaty with the United States during Frei's administration. On the basis of this treaty, the U. S. government through the Agency for International Development (AID), insured nearly all of the new financing provided by the U. S. mining enterprises. The expropriation insurance together with the Export-Import Bank loans indicates that the United States government was committed strongly to the expansion of Chile's copper mining industry.

During 1964-69 Chilean copper policy led to dramatic changes in the direction of its sales abroad (see Table 4. 3). The principal market for Chilean copper in 1964 was the United States (41 percent), followed in descending order of importance by the European Economic Community (EEC) with 28 percent, and the United Kingdom (16. 5 percent). Five years later in 1969, the EEC had become Chile's principal customer (40 percent of copper purchases); and the U. S. share had declined sharply to 17 percent, equal to that of the United Kingdom.

TABLE 4.3

Chilean Copper Exports by Destination, 1964–69
(percent distribution)

	1964	1965	1966	1967	1968	1969
European Economic Community	28.2	34.9	38.0	41.3	34.5	40.4
Germany	12.5	15.7	22.7	21.2	19.6	20.8
France	3.2	3.4	6.1	6.3	5.4	7.7
Italy	3.9	4.7	6.9	8.7	7.8	9.9
United Kingdom	16.5	15.9	17.0	16.1	17.4	17.4
Japan	1.9	2.8	4.3	6.2	8.4	9.3
United States	41.0	37.5	31.4	23.4	25.3	17.2
Other	12.4	8.9	9.3	13.0	14.4	15.7
Total	100.0	100.0	100.0	100.0	100.0	100.0

Source: Private communication, CODELCO.

Japan, which purchased less than two percent of Chile's copper in 1964, increased its share to over nine percent in 1969. The explanation for this dramatic shift in Chile's copper markets lies in the "Chileanization" agreements that provided for a tripling of copper refining capacity from 1965-70. Chilean copper sales to Europe were constrained by Chile's limited capacity to refine the red metal: smelted copper whose ultimate destination was Europe was first sent to the United States for further processing in U.S. refineries. With the buildup of significant refining capacity in Chile in the latter 1960s, European and Japanese customers were able to meet their requirements of refined copper directly from Chile.

ANACONDA AND THE POLITICS OF NATIONALIZATION

The Christian Democratic Party during the summer of 1967 split at the very heart of its organization. "The moderates are banded around an increasingly isolated Frei on the one side, and on the other are the left-wing rebeldes (rebels) who captured control of the Christian Democratic Party apparatus."[37] The Party's political technical committee recommended that the "means of production should belong to the State," and the new party directorate proposed a "noncapitalist method of development."[38] The rebeldes believed in a total break with capitalism and the adoption of a socialist option for development, which they preferred to call "communitarianism." They also stressed "the conflict of interests between Chile, Latin America, and the underdeveloped world, on the one hand, and the developed capitalist world, symbolized by the United States, on the other."[39]

In the spring of 1969, Juan Hamilton, first vice president of the Christian Democrats and a former interior minister, announced that his party would continue to push for "recovering the basic resources of the country." This should be done, he was quoted as saying, "either by the process of Chileanization or by nationalization when it is required."[40] Toward the end of Eduardo Frei's presidential term, a combination of extreme leftists, including members of his party's rebelde faction, mounted a campaign for seizure of U.S. copper holdings.

In the face of the criticism that he had given away too much, the president moved to defuse a potential campaign issue; and in June 1969 negotiated a "progressive nationalization" of the Anaconda Company's two major properties, the Chuquicamata and El Salvador mines. Anaconda made clear, in a separate statement, that it had accepted the offer to nationalize its holdings "to avoid expropriation by the Government of Chile through legislation."[41]

One of the most important political factors affecting the status of Anaconda in Chile was the defection of the Chilean conservative groups to the position of the left-wing parties in the late 1960s. This defection was in sharp contrast to the solid operational support given by business and landowning groups to the U.S. copper mining companies during the early 1950s, which culminated in the "New Deal" Law. The refusal of the Chilean right to come to Anaconda's defense during the critical nationalization negotiations, and more important, during the subsequent expropriation proceedings, was intimately linked to the perceived effects of the Alliance for Progress. Theodore H. Moran aptly summarizes this dynamic relationship,

> We have seen that the land reform proposals of the Alliance for Progress were at the heart of the breakdown in the conservative foreign alliance in Chile. There were other irritants as well: (1) the Alliance envisioned a stiff income tax law and more effective collection procedures, which were broadly unpopular with the conservative groups; and (2) the Alliance offered a source of international funds to both the Alessandri and Frei governments so that neither was as dependent on the U.S. companies for revenues, which weakened the bargaining position of the companies and irritated them. Neither of these

factors, however, was nearly as important as the
Agrarian Reform issue and the consequent struggle
over the right of property. [42]

The proposals of the alliance for agrarian and tax reform, according
to Moran, inspired the Chilean conservative groups to hold the U.S.
companies hostage to get the reforms stopped or mitigated. Failing
to achieve this result, the business and landowning groups joined in
the attack that resulted in the nationalization of Anaconda.

The involuntary sale provided for the acquisition of both
mining properties by the Chilean government in a two-stage arrange-
ment. On 1 January 1970, the Chilean Copper Corporation (CODELCO)
delivered promissory notes totaling $174.5 million as payment for
51 percent of the shares of Chile Exploration Company and Andes
Copper Mining Company, Anaconda's two subsidiaries operating the
Chuquicamata and El Salvador mines, respectively. The purchase
price was based on the book value at that time and payments were to
be made in semiannual installments over 12 years starting 30 June
1970 at six percent tax free interest on the outstanding balance. [43]
It is important to emphasize that the dollar bonds representing the
purchase price for the shares were issued by an authorized agency of
the Chilean government, CODELCO, and guaranteed by Corporacion
de Fomento (the Chilean Development Corporation). Policies of the
two Chilean mixed companies were to be determined by their newly
constituted boards of directors, and Anaconda agreed to provide
operating management services for a minimum of three years for a
fee of one percent of gross sales plus recovery of any expenses
incurred. [44] The Chilean government also contracted to acquire
the remaining 49 percent Anaconda equity "after 1972, but not later
than the end of 1981. "[45] In an address to the nation in which he
explained the terms of the agreement, President Frei stated, "I am
certain that the formula for transfer of foreign investment to national
ownership, without difficulties and useless violence, will be an example and a model that can open a wide road in the relations between the
two Americas. "[46]

The terms for the nationalization of Anaconda's Chilean mining
properties were similar to another agreement reached about the same
time covering acquisition by the Zambian government of a 51 percent
interest in the two major copper mining groups operating in Zambia—
Roan Selection Trust and the Ango-American Corporation. [47] Compensation in Zambia also was based on estimated book values, and payment was made in tax free, government guaranteed bonds denominated
in U.S. dollars bearing an interest rate of six percent. The foreign
mining groups, each of which retained 49 percent of the shares in the

new mixed Zambian companies, agreed to provide management services under contracts that run for a minimum of 10 years.

Concurrently with the nationalization agreement, Anaconda was subjected also to revised taxation agreements whereby the Chilean government would receive a larger share of revenues generated by the rising world price of copper. Subsequently, the Chilean minister of mines announced that a similar understanding had been reached with the Kennecott Copper Corporation. The treasury would receive a larger share of the Gran Mineria's income based on a sliding scale that began once the price of copper rose over 40 cents per pound. [48] The "over-price" tax formula of the early 1950s thus was reintroduced in 1969, despite Chile's pledge made in 1967 to guarantee tax stability for 20 years.

CONCLUDING OBSERVATIONS

The experience of Anaconda and Kennecott in Chile from the mid-1940s to 1970 yields the following significant highlights: (1) Chilean policy toward the U. S.-controlled copper companies (known locally as the Gran Mineria) proved to be highly erratic, shifting between a posture of pragmatic accommodation to the application of onerous and counterproductive tax measures; (2) company responses to these changing climates were highly elastic, that is, decisions to invest, expand output, and engage in exploratory operations were correlated positively with official measures that promised long-run tax stability, moderate tax rates, and security of property.

The Chilean treasury could capture an ever growing share of the Gran Mineria's income—but only at the cost of repelling new foreign investment in copper mining and consequent erosion of the future tax base. Given this short-sighted political orientation and the country's limited market power in the international copper economy, Chile lost at least two excellent opportunities—in the early 1950s and again in the early 1960s—to attract massive foreign direct investments in its key export sector. Instead, heavy taxes, including foreign exchange penalties, and other inhibiting measures induced the U. S. copper companies (which operate on a global scale) to abandon expansion plans in Chile and direct capital funds to less productive mineral sites in other countries offering a more favorable investment climate.

The "New Deal" Law of May 1955, supported by pragmatic nationalists (including influential elements of Chile's business, scientific, and engineering communities) reversed the declining production trend. The U. S. enterprises invested $200 million in copper mining facilities, increased output by one-half, and raised materially the level of Chile's proven copper reserves through their exploratory activities. But beginning around 1961, the investment climate for the Gran Mineria again deteriorated: expropriation of the U.S. companies became a clear possibility; new copper taxes were imposed; company profits were again squeezed; and their ambitious second phase expansion program shelved.

A decisive shift in the mid-1960s of Chile's balance of political power in favor of the Christian Democrats provided the opportunity for a new initiative toward the Gran Mineria. President Frei's "Chileanization" or partnership policy, reflecting the resurgence of pragmatic nationalism, elicited a favorable response from both Anaconda and Kennecott. A $600 million expansion program got underway. Designed to dramatically raise the Gran Mineria's copper production and exports, the program was expected to transform Chile into the world's leading copper exporting nation by 1972.

Chile signed an investment guarantee treaty with the United States during Frei's administration. On the basis of this treaty, the U.S. government insured a major share of the new investments of the U.S. enterprises against expropriation. It is significant to note, however, that the two 20-year tax stabilization agreements concluded between Chile and the U.S. copper mining enterprises in 1955 and 1967 were broken by the government in 1961 and 1969, respectively.

Toward the close of President Eduardo Frei's term as president, the Chilean government had already acquired 51 percent ownership of the largest copper properties—Kennecott's El Teniente and Anaconda's Chuquicamata and El Salvador mines. The latter's smaller Exotica mine was 25 percent Chilean-owned. These ownership shares were acquired by the Chilean government in exchange for dollar repayable notes or bonds that represented a corresponding share of the book value of the U.S.-owned firms. Further, the Chilean government contracted to purchase the remaining 49 percent interest in the large Anaconda mines "after 1972 but not later than the end of 1981." Finally, the three mixed enterprises that operated the El Teniente, Chuquicamata, and El Salvador mines were controlled by the Chilean government through majority representation in their newly constituted boards of directors. Operating services were maintained for the mines through management contracts with both Kennecott and Anaconda. It was in the best interest of Anaconda and Kennecott that the large mines in which they continued to hold a minority position should be well managed. For the successful operation of the mines ultimately would assure the liquidation of the Chilean government's debts to the U.S. mining enterprises.

In conclusion, nationalization with compensation of the U.S.-owned copper mining enterprises was practically an accomplishment in 1970.

NOTES

1. In the mid-1960s Anaconda's Chilean mines accounted for about two-thirds of the company's world copper mining; Kennecott's mine, El Teniente, produced only about one-fourth of the company's overall world total.

2. Oficina de Planificacion Nacional, Antecedentes Sobre el Desarrolo Chileno 1960-70, serie no. 1 (ODEPLAN), Planes Sexenales (Santiago, Chile: Gobierno de Chile, 1971), p. 129.

3. "Some Aspects of the Inflationary Process in Chile," Economic Bulletin for Latin America, United Nations 1, no. 1 (1956): 46.

4. Alberto Cabero, Chile y los Chilenos, segunda edicion (Santiago: Imprenta Cervantes, 1940), p. 321.

5. U.S. Department of the Interior, Mineral Resources of the United States (Washington, D.C.: Government Printing Office, 1926).

6. Joseph Grunwald and Philip Musgrove, Natural Resources in Latin American Development (Baltimore and London: Johns Hopkins Press, 1970), p. 167.

7. "Guia de Estudios de Geografia en Chile," Revista Geografica de Chile 5, nos. 15-16 (1958): 51. Translation by the writer.

8. Thomas G. Sanders, "Chile and its Copper," American Universities Field Staff, West Coast South America Series 26, no. 1 (March, 1969): 13.

9. Hans H. Landsberg, Leonard L. Fischman, and Joseph L. Fisher, Resources in America's Future (Baltimore: Johns Hopkins Press, 1963), p. 453.

10. Chase Manhattan Bank, "The World Copper Trade," Latin American Business Highlights 15, no. 4 (fourth quarter, 1965): 11.

11. According to Orris C. Herfindahl, the leading six companies produced 62.5 percent and the leading eight 70 percent of world copper output in 1956. See Orris C. Herfindahl, Copper Costs and Prices: 1870-1957 (Baltimore: Johns Hopkins Press, 1959), p. 165, table II.

12. See Chase Manhattan Bank, "Report on Copper," World Business (November 1967): 15-16; and (April 1967): 10-12. See also Forbes 1 January 1966, p. 145.

13. Forbes, 15 May 1966, p. 29.

14. Raymond F. Mikesell, "Conflict and Accommodation in Direct Foreign Investment: The Copper Industry," paper presented at the Conference on Latin American-United States Economic Relations, 18-21 March 1973, Austin, Texas, p. 4.

15. The writer is indebted to Frank Masson, formerly on the staff of the Economic Commission for Latin America, for this appropriate phrase.

16. "La Industria de Cobre Revive Gracias a la Nueva Legislacion," Boletin de la Sociedad Cientifica de Chile, Santiago, Chile, 5 (December 1956): 17. Author's translation.

17. The relationship between the rising tax burden and the negative investment/production response was first developed in my article "Taxation of United States-Owned Copper Companies in Chile," National Tax Journal 14, no. 1 (March 1961): 81-87.

18. Saul Arriola, commercial manager, Braden Copper Company. Text of a talk delivered to the International Rotary Club, 19 January 1955, Santiago. An independent study by a Chilean engineer confirms the high tax rate (82.3 percent in 1952) on the Gran Mineria. See Federico Lastra, "Estudio Sobre el Cobre," Revista Chilean de Ingeniera, no. 62 (January-February 1954).

19. Braden Copper Company, Santiago, Chile, "Tax Rates on Copper Production" (mimeographed report); and Lastra, op. cit.

20. For the estimated relationship between hypothetical exchange rates and average production costs see Instituto de Economia, Desarrollo Economico de Chile, 1940-1956 (Santiago, Chile: Editorial del Pacifico, 1957), p. 185.

21. Joseph Grunwald, "Copper" (Washington, D.C.: Resources for the Future, 1967, p. 63, (mimeographed report).

22. Economic Commission for Latin America, Economic Survey of Latin America, 1954 (New York: United Nations, 1955), pp. 26-28.

23. Anaconda Company, "Chuquicamata" (a brochure, no date), p. 9.

24. Instituto de Economia, op. cit., p. 185.

25. "Contribution of Copper to Chilean Economic Development, 1920-1967," in Raymond F. Mikesell, et. al., Foreign Investment in the Petroleum and Mineral Industries (Baltimore and London: Johns Hopkins Press, 1971), p. 415.

26. Grunwald and Musgrove, op. cit., p. 170.

27. Mario Vera Valenzuela, La Politica Economica de Cobre en Chile (Santiago: Ediciones de la Universidad de Chile, 1961).

28. The Economist Intelligence Unit, Ltd., Quarterly Economic Review: Chile, no. 45 (November 1963): 10.

29. U.S. News and World Report, 26 March 1962, p. 110.

30. Russell Watson, "Copper Complexities," Wall Street Journal, 8 September 1964, p. 6.

31. Barron's, 1 April 1963, p. 1.

32. Kennecott would have preferred bringing private Chilean partners into the venture, but local partners were not forthcoming.

See C. E. Michaelson, Joint Mining Ventures Abroad: New Concepts for a New Era, Jacking Award Lecture, The American Institute of Mining, Metallurgical, and Petroleum Engineers, 19 February 1969, Washington, D. C.

33. "Chile Rescata Su Riqueza No. 1 El Cobre," Dece, no. 7 (January 1965): 3.

34. Information received from Banco Central de Chile and CODELCO.

35. Derived from data contained in Oficina de Planificacion Nacional, op. cit., pp. 139-40, tables 96-98.

36. "An Ex-banker Treats Copper's Sickest Giant," Business Week, 19 February 1972, p. 54.

37. Charles J. Parrish, Arpad J. Von Lazar, and Jorge Tapis Videla, The Chilean Congressional Election of March 7, 1965: An Analysis (Washington, D. C.: Institute for the Comparative Study of Political Systems, 1967), p. 28.

38. "Frei Stands Alone in Fight for Free Enterprise," The Times of the Americas, 27 September 1967, p. 4, and Paul E. Sigmund, "Chile: Open Season on President Frei," The Reporter (21 September 1967): 33-35.

39. Thomas G. Sanders, A Note on Chilean Politics, AUFS West Coast South American Series 15, no. 4, (November 1968).

40. Wall Street Journal, May 12, 1969, p. 4.

41. Statement released by the Anaconda Company the evening of 26 June 1969.

42. Theodore H. Moran, "The Alliance for Progress and the Foreign Copper Companies and their Local Conservative Allies in Chile, 1955-1970," Inter-American Economic Affairs 25, no. 4 (Spring 1972): 22.

43. Corporation de Fomento (CORFO), Economic Background Information, no. 13 (July 1969).

44. Statement released by the Anaconda Company the evening of 26 June 1969.

45. CORFO, Chile Economic Notes, no. 54 (5 January 1970).

46. CORFO, Economic Background Information, no. 13 (July 1969).

47. Wall Street Journal, 18 November 1969, p. 7.

48. CORFO, Chile Economic Notes, no. 50 (16 October 1969).

5

THE GAME WITHOUT WINNERS: "INTEGRAL NATIONALIZATION" OF THE U.S. COPPER MINES IN CHILE

The expropriation of the U.S.-owned copper mining enterprises in Chile by the Marxist coalition government led by the late President Salvador Allende Gossens offers a particularly interesting case for study. First, in terms of the magnitude of assets involved, the Chilean case historically represents the most important expropriatory action involving a U.S.-owned industry in Latin America. Including notes repudiated by the Chilean government, assets at stake have a value of between $547 million and $623 million. Second, the measure was carried out through a constitutional amendment approved by the Chilean Congress. Third, the expropriation bill, signed into law on 16 July 1971, as interpreted by President Allende, specifically denied the large U.S. copper mining companies the right of recourse through the regular courts of law to the Chilean Supreme Court.

Anticipating the discussion of Chapter 6, the Chilean government under Allende decided that a constitutional amendment was the only procedure whereby the state could release itself from the bindings placed on it by the "Chileanization" and "Pacted Nationalization" agreements. In brief, the Marxist regime had to "unmake" the work of President Eduardo Frei and insure that the "Integral Nationalization of the large copper mines would not be "exposed to the interminable discussions before regular courts of justice."[1]

This chapter begins with an examination of the Copper Expropriation Amendment viewed in the context of the Chilean presidential election of 1970. It proceeds with an evaluation of President Allende's "excess profits" allegation. A discussion of Anaconda's response to the "rough body blow" struck by Chile is followed by an examination of the postwar economic impact of "Big Mining" on the Chilean economy. The last two sections weigh the costs of "Integral Nationalization" and subsequent politicization of the large copper mines.

THE TERMS OF THE COPPER EXPROPRIATION AMENDMENT

In my paper delivered in January 1968 at the Annual Meeting of the American Institute of Mining, Metallurgical, and Petroleum Engineers, Inc., I concluded with a cautionary note,

> Despite the "Chileanization" and nationalization agreements, some questions remained concerning the future status of the Gran Mineria. Once investments are committed in the form of machinery, equipment, and structures they can be amortized only over a lengthy time span. They become, in effect, victims of a future regime which may decide not to honor agreements concluded by a preceding government. [2]

Of the three candidates for the Chilean presidence—Radomiro Tomic, the Christian Democrat contender; Salvador Allende, representing the Marxist coalition; and Jorge Alessandri, the independent rightist—only the latter was prepared to accept the remaining "Chileanization" or partnership agreements. Alessandri campaigned on the same platform that he had supported as president in the 1958-64 period: free enterprise, encouragement of foreign investment, and a minimum of state interference. Tomic, accepting his party's new "political declaration and program base," agreed that his Christian Democratic government "would continue the process of recuperation of our basic riches started during the present government, and would complete by law the nationalization of all the principal copper producers."[3]

The election plurality* and ultimate victory of Salvador Allende, the candidate of Unidad Popular (embracing Communists,

---

* Allende won a small plurality with 36.3 percent of the votes cast over highly respected but aging expresident Jorge Alessandri (34.9 percent) and Radomiro Tomic, who received only 27.8 percent. Because Allende did not secure a majority of the total vote, the congress exercised its constitutional mandate to select Allende or Alessandri. In accordance with its custom, the congress on 24 October elected the plurality winner, 153-35. For further details see James

Socialists, Radicals, and Independent Leftists) foreclosed any arrangements with the large U.S. copper companies other than expropriation.

The Allende administration took office on 4 November 1970 for a six-year term and on 22 December 1970 the president submitted to the Chilean Congress a constitutional reform bill to permit the expropriation of the mineral resources and related facilities of the large copper companies. On 11 July 1971 a joint session of the congress unanimously voted to ratify the reform bill; and on 16 July, following the president's signature, the bill became law.

The refusal of the Chilean right to come to the U.S. companies' defense during the expropriation proceedings was intimately linked, as noted in the previous chapter, to the perceived effects of the Alliance for Progress. The proposals of the Alliance for agrarian and tax reform inspired the Chilean conservative groups to hold the U.S. enterprises hostage to have the reforms stopped or mitigated. Failing to achieve this result, the business and landowning groups joined in the attack that resulted in the de facto uncompensated expropriation of Anaconda and Kennecott in 1971. Leading conservative landowners, businessmen, and politicians reasoned that if Chileans could be deprived of their property without adequate compensation, so could foreign investors.

The constitutional amendment (Law 17.450) provided that the mixed enterprises formed by the Chilean government through its Chilean Copper Corporation (CODELCO) and U.S. mining companies in Chile be nationalized and that all mineral resources of the joint ventures become the property of the state. The nationalization law provided for the following:[4]

1. Compensation of properties taken, excluding mineral resources, on the basis of book value as determined by the comptroller general. Payment to be made in 30-year bonds at no less than three percent per annum.

2. Authority to the president to make a series of deductions from value of compensation including alleged "excess profits" earned by the U.S. companies between 1955-70. (This provision, however, was permissive rather than obligatory.)

3. Debts of the mixed enterprises guaranteed by the Chilean government during President Frei's administration not to be assumed unless the proceeds were deemed to be "invested usefully" in the judgment of President Allende.

L. Busey, <u>Latin American Political Guide</u> (Manitou Springs, Colorado: Juniper Editions, 1973), pp. 21-22.

4. Appeal of the comptroller general's decision with a period of 15 days before a five-man Special Copper Tribunal set up for this purpose, constituted of two jurists and three government officials appointed by President Allende.

TABLE 5.1

Valuation by Comptroller General of Chile of the Gran Mineria as a Basis for Compensation, 31 December 1970 (millions of U.S. dollars)

	Book Value	U.S. Companies' Share	
		(percent)	
Anaconda			
Chuquicamata	242.0	49	118.6
El Salvador	68.4	49	33.5
Exotica	14.8	75	11.1
Kennecott			
El Teniente	318.3	49	156.0
Cerro Corporation			
Andina	20.1	70	14.1
Total	663.6		333.3

Source: Derived from Wolfgang G. Friedmann, et al., 1972 Supplement to Cases and Materials on International Law (St. Paul, Minnesota: West Publishing Company, 1972), pp. 150-51.

Decree 92 of the Ministry of Mines establishes the rationale for the "excess profits" deduction.[5] Article 7 of the decree states that the president may "deduct excess profits obtained by the foreign companies (my emphasis) as a way to restitute to the nation the legitimate participation which it should have received from these natural resources."[6] And article 8 stipulates that in making those deductions from the value of compensation due to the U.S. copper companies, the president should, above all other considerations, respect "the spiritual and the historical-political inspiration" of the constitutional reform.[7]

On 11 October the comptroller general of the Republic, Hector Humeres, submitted his assessment of the large copper mines as of the end of 1970 at $664 million (see Table 5.1). About one-half of this amount ($333 million) represented the remaining equity of the U.S. enterprises. Meanwhile, on 28 September President Allende set the amount of "excess profits" that would be deducted from compensation to be paid to the U.S. copper mining companies at $774 million—according to his calculations, profits allegedly received over 12 percent of book value from 5 May 1955 (the date of the "New Deal" Law) and 31 December 1970. On this accounting, Kennecott had earned "excess profits" of $410 million and Anaconda, $364 million. This deduction alone was to transform the U.S. copper mining companies from creditors to debtors. Their assets and future earning prospects were wiped out in a single political act. Excess profits were not charged against large new mines that were becoming operational in 1970: Cerro Corporation's Andina and Anaconda's Exotica.

EVALUATION OF PRESIDENT ALLENDE'S "EXCESS PROFITS" ALLEGATION

In his speech delivered at the United Nations General Assembly, President Allende said, "We want everybody to understand this clearly: We have not confiscated the great foreign copper-mining companies."[8] Further, he stated that,

> The profits which some of the nationalized companies had obtained over the previous 15 years were so exorbitant that, in applying the limit of a reasonable profit of 12 percent per annum, the companies were affected by significant deductions. Such was the case, for example, with a branch of the Anaconda Company, whose annual profits in Chile between 1955 and 1970 averaged 21.5 percent on its book value, while Anaconda's profits in other countries were only 3.6 percent per annum. The same applied in the case of a branch of the Kennecott Copper Corporation which, over the same period made an average annual profit of 52.8 percent in Chile, even reaching such incredible rates as 106 percent in 1967, 113 percent in 1968, and over 205 percent in 1969.[9]

By way of answering President Allende's allegations, Anaconda contends that the cumulative profits of its Chilean operations over the 16 years, 1955-70, resulted in an average annual income of $29,698,175 (or $475 million for the period).[10] Relating the annual profit to the company's annual average consolidated net worth in Chile for the same period ($415 million), results in an overall return of 7.15 percent on investment.

While not revealing the actual rate of return on its investments in Chile, Kennecott claims that for the same period net earnings before taxes on its equity in El Teniente were 32 percent higher than that for its U. S. mines. However, net earnings after taxes for El Teniente were 45 percent below Kennecott's domestic mines' earnings. The company concludes,

> Not in any year since 1955 did El Teniente earn more after taxes or on investment than Kennecott's domestic operations. The Chilean allegation, therefore, has no validity or foundation. [11]

The following discussion will attempt to reconcile the widely differing interpretations of the Chilean government and the U. S. copper mining enterprises regarding the latter's profits.

First, it must be noted that the U. S. copper mining enterprises earned their profits in compliance with Chilean law and the terms of specific tax agreements concluded in 1955 and 1967. Their operations were monitored closely by the Chilean government. The deductions made for "excess profits" penalize the companies for acts that previous Chilean administrations officially approved. Since it is stated nowhere that the alleged "excess profits" are based on the violation of Chilean law, President Allende's administration has effectively abrogated 16 years of tax legislation.

The second point is economic rather than legal and reflects on the accuracy of President Allende's calculations. Table 5.2 reveals the profits of the U. S. copper subsidiaries after payment of Chilean taxes between May 1955 and 1970. Thus, the actual accumulated profits for the period of 15 and two-thirds years, totaled $1,002 million. Subtracting from this figure the alleged "excess profits" of $774 million leaves a balance of "normal profits" totaling $228 million, or $14.5 million per year ($228 million divided by 15 and two-thirds). Capitalizing this average annual "normal profit" at 12 percent (Allende's "reasonable profit" rate) results in an average net worth of $121 million of the U. S. copper mining companies—a figure that falls dramatically short of my own estimate of the average U. S. equity for the 16-year period ($540 million) and the book value estimated by the comptroller general of Chile as the basis for compensation: $333.2 million.

In calculating the book value (net assets) of the Gran Mineria, I have accepted the estimate of depreciated assets given by C.W. Reynolds for yearend 1959 (see Table 5.2) and added to this estimate the annual net direct investments by the Gran Mineria through the end of 1970. The equity of the U. S.-owned copper mining companies was reduced in 1967 by $92.7 million (Kennecott's transfer of ownership of 51 percent in the El Teniente mine) and by $174 million at the beginning of 1970 (Anaconda's sale of 51 percent in the Chuquicamata and El Salvador mines).

TABLE 5.2

The Gran Mineria: Net Assets, Profits, and Rate of Return, 1944-70
(millions of U.S. dollars)

Year	Net Assets[a]	Net Investments	Nationalized Assets	U.S. Equity (net assets)	Net Profits[b]	Rate of Return (percent)[c]
1944	305.0	—	—	—	17.4	5.7
1945	309.7	—	—	—	11.4	3.6
1946	313.5	—	—	—	21.6	6.8
1947	311.5	—	—	—	36.0	11.5
1948	326.0	—	—	—	48.3	14.8
1949	338.0	—	—	—	26.1	7.7
1950	336.4	—	—	—	30.2	8.9
1951	367.4	—	—	—	38.8	10.5
1952	411.2	—	—	—	34.9	8.4
1953	439.4	—	—	—	13.1	2.9
1954	481.5	—	—	—	18.8	3.9
1955	464.4	—	—	—	54.4	11.7
1956	427.1	—	—	—	75.4	17.6
1957	547.8	—	—	—	37.9	6.9
1958	570.2	—	—	—	27.3	4.7
1959	595.8	25.3	—	—	55.9	9.3
1960	621.1	-22.5	—	—	47.8	7.7
1961	598.6	- 5.5	—	—	37.3	6.2
1962	604.1	- 5.6	—	—	43.5	7.2
1963	598.5	-15.3	—	—	39.3	6.6
1964	582.2	-20.0	—	—	48.1	8.3
1965	562.2	-35.0	—	—	43.9	7.8
1966	527.2	-34.0	—	—	81.9	15.6
1967	493.2	32.0	-92.7	432.5	124.4	28.7
1968	525.2	59.0	—	491.5	125.7	25.6
1969	584.2	56.0	—	547.5	109.2	19.9
1970	640.2	89.0	-174.5	462.0	68.5	14.8
1971	729.2					

[a]Depreciated assets. Net assets and U.S. equity are equal between 1944 and 1966.

[b]Profits of the U.S. subsidiaries after Chilean taxes.

[c]Net profits as a percentage of U.S. equity.

Sources: For value of assets, 1944-59, C.W. Reynolds, "Chile and Copper," in M. Mamalakis and C.W. Reynolds, Essays in the Chilean Economy (New Haven: Yale University Economic Growth Center, 1965), pp. 383-86. For net investment, 1959-70, IMF, Balance of Payments Yearbook, vols. 16, 21, 23 (preliminary) (Washington, D.C.: International Monetary Fund, 1965, 1970, and 1972). For net profits, 1944-64, Banco Central de Chile, Balanza de Pagos de Chile 1964 (Santiago: Banco Central de Chile, 1966), p. 32; and for 1965-70, Banco Central de Chile figures cited in Cobre: Antecedentes Economicos y Estadisticos Relacionados con la Gran Mineria del Cobre, published by the Information Office of the Chilean Senate, 26 January 1971.

On the basis of data given in table 5.2, the average rate of return (net profits as a percent of U.S. equity) for the 1955-70 period was 12.4 percent—hardly an excessive rate for the mineral extraction sector—and roughly equal to the "reasonable profit" cited by Allende. The profit rate varied between 7.2 percent in 1961-65 and 20.9 percent in 1966-70, the latter reflecting a sharp rise in world copper prices.

We may infer from the foregoing discussion that the late President Allende's "excess profits" allegation is without empirical foundation.

ANACONDA: "A ROUGH BODY BLOW"

Before the expropration of its remaining interests in Chile, the Anaconda Company was the largest copper mining enterprise in the non-Communist world. The company's market value fell from $1.4 billion in the latter part of 1969 to a mere $260 million three years later.

In the view of the company, the Allende government, "recognizing there was no other way to deprive Anaconda of its properties and contractual rights under traditional Chilean law without payment of prompt, adequate and effective compensation, devised a fraudulent facade of legality through a special project of constitutional reform."[12] Company officials declared that Anaconda paid $320 million for mines and claims 56 years ago and proceeded to develop the properties into "by far the largest single contributor to the Chilean economy." Anaconda also noted that all contract rights established under the laws of Chile on 31 December 1969, covering the relationship between the company and the Chilean government (that is, the nationalization agreements) have been declared null and void. Further, the company noted that Chile still owed Anaconda $153 million in the form of promissory notes received by the company for the 51 percent interest purchased by Chile 31 December 1969 in the Chuquicamata and El Salvador mines.[13] John Place, who became the company's chief executive in August 1971, characterized Chile's expropriatory act as "a rough body blow that took away two-thirds of our copper production and three-fourths of our earnings."[14] President Place, formerly a vice president with Chase Manhattan Bank, initiated a number of reforms designed to help the company recover from its heavy losses in Chile. He cut Anaconda's New York corporate staff by one-half and reduced the company's work force throughout the United States, for a $25 million a year saving in employment costs alone. And he declared a massive $348.5 million tax write-off related to the loss of the Chilean properties that could be applied against Anaconda's future profits.[15]

Chile signed an investment guarantee treaty with the United States during the Frei administration. On the basis of this treaty, the U.S. government, through the Agency for International Development (AID), insured a share of the additional investments of the U.S. copper companies against expropriation. In 1967 AID issued contracts of guarantee covering investments made by Anaconda and its Chilean subsidiaries in new and expanding mining operations and earnings subsequently accumulated on those investments. The most important of these policies affected equity investments in the Chuquicamata and El Salvador properties.[16] For the first two years of the contracts, Anaconda elected standby rather than current coverage. At the close of 1969 the Chilean government, at its insistence, nationalized the Chuquicamata and El Salvador properties by purchasing 51 percent of the equity and contracted to acquire the remaining 49 percent interest. AID took the position that it no longer considered its contracts to be in effect (1) "in view of the fact that Anaconda had previously elected standby rather than current coverage for the period when the relevant events occurred,"[17] and (2) because a 51 percent disinvestment had occurred, thereby transforming Anaconda's share into a minority interest in a government-controlled enterprise, fundamentally changing its character.

It is Anaconda's position, on the other hand, that the 1969 transactions did not affect its right to elect coverage in subsequent contract years.[18] In December 1969 and again in December 1970, Anaconda attempted to elect to carry full expropriation coverage for the succeeding annual contract periods and tendered premiums. The premiums were in each case not accepted by AID, but the agency agreed that it would not dispute the proper tender of premiums by Anaconda if the company prevailed on its claim to coverage. The company's insurance claims for the recovery of expropriation losses in Chile total $154 million.

The Overseas Private Investment Corporation (OPIC), an independent U.S. government agency, succeeded to the rights and obligations of AID's private investment guarantee and support functions in January 1971. OPIC denied Anaconda's claims for its former Chuquicamata and El Salvador mines on the ground that the company's insurance was not in force at the time of nationalization in 1969.[19] At the same time, in September 1972, the Anaconda Company received payment of $11.9 million from OPIC to cover loss of its equity investment in the Exotica copper mine. Investment insurance contracts provide for arbitration in any matters of dispute in accordance with the rules of the American Arbitration Association.

It would appear, on hindsight, that Anaconda's heavy commitment to one country of investments and managerial-technical resources has proved less than prudent. Good profit opportunities associated with low-cost production costs in Chilean mines should have been balanced more carefully against Chile's political climate, and the related shifts in policy, and the "rules of the game" by which the U. S. copper companies were allowed to play. As one Anaconda director observed, "The company was big in metallurgical, geological, and scientific skills, but somewhat weaker in the financial and business judgment end."[20]

THE GRAN MINERIA'S IMPACT ON THE CHILEAN ECONOMY

On 25 January 1971, the Chilean Copper Corporation (CODELCO), an agency of the Chilean government, published a full-page advertisement in the New York Times on the forthcoming expropriation of the large copper mines in Chile. The advertisement, designed to justify this measure, sought to discredit the U. S. copper mining companies operating in Chile and belittled their contribution to the Chilean economy. In a summary passage the burden of Chile's underdevelopment is placed on U. S. direct investments,

> The conclusion is clear: in a little over a half a century these U. S. companies took out from our country an amount greater than that created by Chileans in terms of industries, highways, cities, ports, schools, hospitals, trade, etc., during our country's entire history.
>   This is the basic cause of our underdevelopment. The basic cause of our meager industrial growth, of our primitive agriculture, unemployment, low wages our very low standard of life, the high rate of infant mortality, and it is the cause of our poverty and backwardness.[21]

The U. S. copper mining companies are held responsible for "substantial and permanent decapitalization of the national economy." CODELCO also takes the Gran Mineria to task for its failure to keep up with world copper production, thus, according to the advertisement, "while world copper production increased by 31 percent in the period 1960-1969, Chilean production increased by only 27 percent. . . ." The responsibility for Chile's diminishing share of world copper output over a two-decade period is assigned uniquely to Anaconda and Kennecott. The CODELCO advertisement also observes that Chile contains positively known copper reserves totaling 37 million tons, the largest of any country in the world. However, the report is silent on the role of the U. S. companies, particularly Anaconda, in greatly expanding Chile's proven copper reserves.

How valid are the foregoing charges and allegations when applied to the Gran Mineria? In evaluating the impact of the U. S. copper mining enterprises on the Chilean economy we will again apply the analytical framework developed in Chapter 2.

It is clear that the total benefit of the Gran Mineria to the Chilean economy has been much higher in the postwar period than in earlier times. For one thing, the transference of skills and technical knowledge to Chile increased per dollar invested. Anaconda and Kennecott trained and employed a much higher percentage of Chileans in technical and administrative positions after World War II, and numerous employees who have benefitted from the Gran Mineria's training programs have joined other enterprises in Chile in important posts. The second reason is the rise in the "returned value" to Chile per dollar of output of the U. S. mining enterprises: greater percentage of taxes; higher wages and fringe benefits; and a greater share of supplies, materials, and services purchased within the host country.

The share of total value returned to Chile by the U. S. copper mining companies rose from about 40 percent in the 1920s to about 80 percent in the period 1960-70.[22] From the 1920s to 1960, when Chile's real gross domestic product grew at a sluggish 2.7 percent annually, the value returned from copper produced by the U. S.-owned mines increased by more than 5 percent a year.[23] Thus, even before the imposition of nationalization and expropriation measures, Chile had succeeded in integrating the copper industry into the national economy and reducing its isolated character.

Information supplied to the author by the Anaconda Company shows that its Chilean subsidiaries returned 80.4 percent of the value of total copper production to the host country, including $1 billion in tax revenue during the two-decade period 1949-68. Returned values included, in addition to Chilean taxes, local operational outlays and net investments. The nonreturned values comprised dividends sent to the parent company (11.2 percent of total sales value) and expenses incurred abroad (8.4 percent of sales), mainly shipping and insurance.[24] Data supplied by the Kennecott Corporation also indicate the contribution of the company's subsidiaries to the Chilean economy. The gross income of Kennecott's El Teniente mine in the 55-year period of 1916-70 amounted to $3,430,000,000. Of that sum, $2,491,000,000 (or 72.6 percent) remained in Chile, $430 million (12.5 percent) was expended outside Chile for imports of machinery, materials, supplies, and services, and $509 million (or 14.8 percent of sales) constituted profits.[25] My own calculations, derived from statistics of Chile's Banco Central (see Table 4.1), corroborate the view that Gran Mineria operations have resulted in large net benefits for Chile. During the 25-year postwar period 1946-70, Chile retained 77 percent of the value of copper produced by the large mines.

The 11,000 Anaconda workers and employees, who with their families made up about 60,000 people, received in wages and benefits many times more than the amount paid to workers in similar occupations in Chile.[26] Elaborate educational, medical, and recreational services provided by Anaconda for mining community members have resulted in a significant lowering of infant mortality rates—to a level about equal to that of the United States[27]—and literacy standards sharply above those prevailing in the rest of Chile. The city of Chuquicamata (population 30,000) was served by a 240-bed company hospital built in 1960—one of the finest in all of Latin America. Its staff was composed entirely of Chilean doctors, nurses, and technicians. Kennecott's 165-bed Sewell Hospital included on its staff 22 doctors, 4 pharmacists, and 30 university-trained nurses. The cost-free medical care made available by Kennecott to the more than 27,000 eligible members helped to reduce infant mortality in the Sewell mining community to 34 per 1,000 in 1970, compared with the national average of 79.[28]

Foreign investment may play an important role in the development of national entrepreneurs. This role, summarized by Paul Rosenstein-Rodan, aptly describes the contribution of the U.S. copper companies in Chile,

> By training, hiring and promoting national managers, and by its "demonstration effect" it contributes to their growth in quantity and quality. Many of those managers may grow into future independent national entrepreneurs and may be capable of participating in or taking over the management of foreign subsidiaries when in the future they pass into majority national ownership. A stimulus is finally given to national entrepreneurship by the creation of new national investment opportunities through subcontracting for deliveries ("backward linkage").[29]

Numerous persons in Chile benefitted from the Gran Mineria's management training programs and assistance to local universities and technical institutes. For example, the first metallurgy curriculum in Chile was established at the University of Conception with Kennecott's help. Through the years, a framework of experienced and efficient Chilean technically trained personnel has grown up within the Gran Mineria: some of these joined other enterprises in Chile in important posts. Kennecott was one of the founders of ICARE, the Chilean equivalent of the American Management Association, which was established to facilitate the introduction of modern management methods and practices in Chile. Prior to the September 1970 presidential elections in Chile, the El Teniente mixed enterprise had 570 in its key management and supervisory group, of which only two were U. S. citizens. According to Kennecott,

> This group of managers and supervisors, predominantly Chilean, gave El Teniente sufficient depth of qualified personnel in the middle and lower management levels. This made it possible for El Teniente, when the mass exodus of supervisors began after September 1970, to make the third and fourth replacements in most key positions, before this supply of trained personnel also disappeared as a result of the large number of resignations which ensued. [30]

The Gran Mineria created important "backward linkage" effects in relation to dozens of Chilean firms through its purchases of foundry materials, railroad and casting equipment, powder, and large varieties of supplies. In the latter 1950s the U. S. companies adopted policies to encourage and assist local manufacturers in developing products imported previously from the United States or Europe. Thus acquisitions in Chile by the Gran Mineria increased from $25.7 million in 1958 to $88.5 million in 1969. [31] In 1967 Anaconda's purchases in Chile amounted to $52.6 million, up from $25.6 million in 1958;[32] and Kennecott's purchases of materials, supplies, and operating equipment made in Chile increased from $4 million in 1955 to more than $20 million in 1969. [33] The local supplier firms were helped by the U. S. mining enterprises to establish standards and quality controls for their products and provided with technical information concerning methods of production.

The strength and growth of an economy depends greatly on the accumulation and modernization of its real capital. During the two decades 1949-68 Anaconda's new investments in Chile reached nearly $500 million. The capital outlays included a sulphide ore treatment plant built during the years 1949-53 at a cost of over $130 million, the expansion of the Chuquicamata open-pit mine, and the development of two new mines. Net investments by Anaconda's Chilean subsidiaries ($499 million new investments less $308 million amortization) during the 20-year period therefore amounted to over $190 million. [34] Significantly, Anaconda reinvested 60 percent of its net profits in Chile in the period 1930-59. [35] The share of investment expenditures made in Chile increased substantially between the 1940s and the 1960s as the economy became able to supply more of the equipment, materials, and services required by the Anaconda and Kennecott subsidiaries. For example, of the $575 million invested from

1967-70 in the copper mining expansion program, $306 million or 60 percent was spent within Chile. [36]

The Kennecott Copper Corporation purchased the El Teniente property from the Guggenheim interests in 1915 and through additional capital outlays increased the mine's annual productive capacity from 16,000 tons in 1916 to 180,000 tons by 1967. This represented a 4.9 percent annual expansion in capacity compared with a 2.7 percent annual growth rate in world copper production. [37] El Teniente was the first Chilean copper mine developed on a modern commercial scale, that is, by application of the principle of mass production to lowgrade ores. All earnings of El Teniente during the formative stage of the property's development, from 1906-27, were reinvested to raise production, with no dividends to its owners.

Chilean copper production, as we have noted, was scheduled to increase substantially faster than world production during the period 1967-72, when the Investment Expansion Program associated with the "Chileanization" agreements was in effect. By pointing to the year 1969, the CODELCO advertisement conveniently eliminated from consideration the delayed production response from the Gran Mineria's investment projects that were scheduled to come on stream during 1971-72.

PERFORMANCE OF THE MINES AFTER EXPROPRIATION

When President Allende took office in November 1970 the investment expansion program of the Gran Mineria was nearly completed. Over the four-year period 1967-70 there was a realized investment of $576 million in the large mines or 96 percent of the amount authorized ($602 million) for the expansion program. [38] The new administration, it would appear, was to become the chief beneficiary of the "Chileanization" agreements concluded in 1966-67 between former President Eduardo Frei and the U.S. copper mining enterprises.

In view of the large expansion in Chile's copper mining capacity, how has expropriation affected the performance of the mines? A comparison of actual results with projected output is given in Table 5.3. The production shortfall of 377,000 tons, or 39 percent of 1972 projected output, was particularly evident in the older mines—Chuquicamata, Exotica, and El Teniente.

What explanation can be offered for such a disappointing performance? Why has the massive growth in physical capacity yielded such a low output? The main reasons for the poor results appear to be the following:

TABLE 5.3

Chile's Gran Mineria: Actual and Projected Production, 1972
(metric tons)

	Actual (b)	Projected (c)	Difference (c-b)
Anaconda Company*	234,643	390,000	-155,357
Chuquicamata	31,271	112,500	- 81,229
Exotica	82,777	110,000	- 27,223
El Salvador			
Kennecott Copper Corp.*			
El Teniente	190,618	280,000	- 89,382
Cerro Corp.*			
Andina	53,910	77,500	- 23,590
Total	593,219	970,000	-376,781

*Before expropriation.

Source: For projected production see Table 4.2. For actual
production, see Republica de Chile, Direccion de Presupuestos,
Exposicion sobre el Estado de la Hacienda Publica, no. 124 (October
1973): 55, table II.

1. An exodus of over 400 Chilean[39] supervisors and technicians and about 150 American and other expatriates in managerial or
technical positions.

2. The replacement of qualified personnel with large numbers
of persons without any previous experience in the copper mining industry.

3. Severe industrial relations problems arising out of the politicization of the mining enterprises and the Chilean Copper Corporation (CODELCO).*

4. The difficulty of maintaining the flow of hundreds of thousands of spare parts to keep the mines and related facilities in good
working order.

---

*It is interesting to note that in February 1973 the workers at
the Chuquicamata mine ended 30 years of Marxist domination of their
union, electing a majority of more than two-to-one from President
Allende's political opposition to the union's board of directors.

Norman Gall, who visited the large Chuquicamata mine in February 1972, observed that "the professional or supervisory payroll was swollen by swarms of new nontechnical personnel, such as sociologists and psychologists and public relations men who plunged into political work on behalf of Unidad Popular or infantile rivalries among themselves."[40] David Silverman, the new Communist manager of the mining complex, told Gall, "There are few people who know about copper and have the government's confidence."[41]

The departure of Chile's most competent supervisors and technicians and their replacement with political appointees and the growing reluctance of the unionized copper workers—these and other factors sharply increased unit production costs in the expropriated mines. One authoritative confidential source calculated the average cost of 45 cents per pound of copper produced in the large mines in 1971. This should be compared with the price obtained by Chile of 49 cents per pound in that year.[42] A study of costs of production in the copper industries in Chile and other major producing countries reports that in 1969, before expropriation, the average cost of production was only 24.3 cents per pound in Chile.[43] Joaquin Figueroa, who served as general manager of the new Andina mine until August 1971, noted,

> Nationalization was justified partly on the grounds of increased revenue for Chile. But even though not a penny was spent on compensation, the mines are paying less than under the Yankee imperialists.[44]

THE COSTS OF "VIOLENT NATIONALIZATION"

The constitutional amendment signed into law on 16 July 1971 produced far-reaching consequences affecting both the U. S. mining enterprises and the Chilean economy. An economic evaluation of the expropriatory action is rendered most appropriately in the perspective of the "Chileanization" and "pacted nationalization" agreements concluded during the latter 1960s.

In Chapter 4 we noted that toward the end of President Eduardo Frei's term as president, nationalization of the large U. S.-owned copper mines was practically accomplished. Significantly, "Chileanization" and "pacted nationalization" were accomplished with the agreement (reluctantly in the case of Anaconda) of the U. S. enterprises and with compensation in dollar-repayable obligations. It was anticipated that the large and growing framework of Chilean supervisors and technicians (trained with the assistance of the U. S. firms) eventually would take complete responsibility for the management of the Gran Mineria. A major investment expansion program designed nearly to double Chile's copper mining capacity was near completion on Allende's assumption of presidential office. Under Frei's administration, Chile attracted generous U. S. economic assistance; and the international financial community also favored the South American nation.

In short, the long range Chilean goal to gain ownership and control over its large copper mines was by 1970 an ineluctable conclusion. Under Eduardo Frei, however, this aim was being furthered (1) without alienating the international financial community and (2) concurrently with a massive expansion of Chile's copper mining capacity. When President Frei went to the Chuquicamata mine in July 1969, he told workers why he had chosen "pacted nationalization" as opposed to the "violent nationalization" urged on him by his Marxist opposition. He explained that the latter approach would have brought Chile into conflict with the copper companies and possibly with the U. S. government. He added, "If we would have broken the law, we would have done things in an unjust way. The outside world would have cut its credits to Chile and the people who are investing would have said, 'How are we going to continue working in Chile if laws or contracts are not respected in that country?'"[45]

Estimates of capital losses sustained by Anaconda and Kennecott in Chile are given in Table 5.4. The total capital loss of each U. S. mining company as of 1973 includes its equity in the Chilean mixed enterprise, plus the unpaid balance on the obligations repudiated by the Chilean government, less the insurance coverage for expropriation issued by OPIC. Depending on whether we accept the U. S. firm's valuation of equity or that of the Chilean comptroller general, Anaconda's capital loss is in the range of $320-304 million and that of Kennecott, $217-156 million. Both of these firms have taken tax write-offs in the United States on their noninsured capital losses in Chile. A part of the cost of the Chilean expropriations has been passed on to the American people directly through congressional replenishment of OPIC's insurance reserve and indirectly through a future reduction in taxes flowing into the U. S. treasury.

However, it may be asked fairly, "Hasn't the U. S. loss been matched by Chile's gain?" The answer would appear to be, "This was a game that had no winners." For one thing, President Frei's warning regarding the option of "violent nationalization" given in 1969 proved to be prophetic. The uncompensated expropriation of the U. S. copper mining investments brought Chile into conflict with both the American-based companies and the U. S. government (see Chapter 6). The lesson, if there is one, in the relations between the United States and the Allende government is, in the words of Paul E. Sigmund, "that a government which is determined to nationalize U. S. companies

TABLE 5.4

Anaconda and Kennecott: Estimated Losses from Expropriation of
Chile's Copper Mines
(millions of U.S. dollars)

U.S. Company Interests	Anaconda		Kennecott	
	Company's Valuation	Chilean Government's Valuation	Company's Valuation	Chilean Government's Valuation
Equity in mixed companies	178.9	163.2	216.9	156.0
Repubidated Chilean CODELCO obligations (unpaid balance)	152.8	152.8	74.7	74.7
Gross company interests	331.7	316.0	291.6	230.7
Less: OPIC coverage	- 11.9[a]	- 11.9[a]	- 74.7[b]	- 74.7[b]
Net company interests (maximum loss)	319.8	304.1	216.9	156.9

[a]Settled by OPIC in September 1972. Excludes $154 million additional coverage in dispute between OPIC and Anaconda.

[b]Settled by OPIC in January 1973.

Sources: For Chilean government valuation, see Table 5.1. Information received from Anaconda Company in response to the author's specific questions. Letter received from Frank R. Milliken, President of Kennecott Copper Corp., 27 October 1971. For OPIC coverage and settlement arrangements, see Topics, Overseas Private Investment Corp. 2, no. 1 (January 1973).

without compensation and to carry out an internal program which effectively destroys its ability to earn foreign exchange cannot expect to receive a subsidy to do so from either the U.S. government or from U.S. private banks."[46] This action damaged Chile's credit with the International Bank for Reconstruction and Development (The World Bank) and the Inter-American Development Bank.

In remarks prepared for delivery to the International Center for Settlement of Investment Disputes, World Bank president Robert S. McNamara warned less developed countries that a "disquieting" trend by governments to annul agreements with foreign investors would "seriously imperil" their credit worthiness and inhibit investment in their entire region.[47] Whether it was due to its poor credit rating (following Allende's declaration of a moratorium on Chile's external debt in November 1972) or its uncompensated takeovers of foreign-owned properties, the Marxist government did not receive any additional credits from either the World Bank or the Inter-American Development Bank. However, Chile did receive disbursements from loans approved earlier by these institutions. A few weeks after McNamara's remarks, in October 1971, Allende's government used the joint annual meeting of the World Bank and the International Monetary Fund as a forum to criticize the bank's lending policies. The head of Chile's delegation to the joint meeting, Central Bank president Alfonso Inestroza charged that the bank could not regard itself as a multilateral institution if "what is actually done in practice appears to indicate that international financial instruments are being used for the foreign policy ends of a particular country."[48] The World Bank, he added, "cannot be an instrument of bilateral policy for any of its member countries." Inestroza's allegations were patently unfair, for the World Bank is enjoined under its articles to suspend loans to a country whose credit is impaired by "the existence of a dispute over a default on its foreign debt or over compensation for foreign-owned property which has been expropriated. . . ."[49] Hence, the bank will not accommodate a member country until the expropriating government engages in a serious effort to reach a fair and equitable settlement and takes steps to see "that there are good prospects that the matter will be cleared up satisfactorily."[50]

Toward the close of Frei's administration, the Chilean government was playing its cards very effectively. Its growing ownership participation in the large mines together with the application of an "overprice tax" assured that Chile would derive maximum benefit from the economic rent of its premier mineral resource. With the enlarged capacity of 970,000 metric tons of copper targeted for 1971-72, the Chilean government would have captured the predominant share of the Gran Mineria's estimated $535 million surplus (profit before taxes). * The larger revenues accruing to Chile from the expanded output of its previously efficient large copper mines could, under a politically moderate regime, have financed easily the compensation required to complete the last phase of the Gran Mineria's nationalization.

Instead, under the ideologically inspired Allende administration, Chile's international credit standing was impaired, mine output remained far short of targeted production capacity, and, with unit costs escalating, the surplus of copper revenues over costs virtually disappeared. "Human capital"—the large framework of Chilean managers and technicians trained by Anaconda and Kennecott—was lost to the nation. Finally, the deterioration of the economy, resulting in part from these factors, was a major element leading to the military coup of 11 September 1973.

NOTES

1. Eduardo Novoa Monreal, La Nacionalizacion del Cobre: Comentarios y Documentos (Santiago: Empresa Editora Nacional Quimantu, 1972), p. 176.

2. Proceedings of the Council of Economics (New York: AIMMPE, 1968), p. 251.

3. The Times of the Americas, March 5, 1970, p. 1.

4. See Wolfgang G. Friedmann, et al., 1972 Supplement to Cases and Materials on International Law (St. Paul, Minn.: West Publishing Co., 1972), pp. 146-49.

5. The decree is reproduced in Monreal, op. cit., appendix 7.

6. Ibid., p. 443 (author's translation)

7. Ibid., pp. 443-44.

8. Speech delivered by Salvador Allende, President of the Republic of Chile, 4 December 1972, before the General Assembly of the United Nations, p. 11.

9. Ibid.

10. Information received from the Anaconda Company in response to specific questions raised by the author.

11. Kennecott Copper Corp., Expropriation of El Teniente, 1971, p. 51.

12. The Anaconda Co., "Anaconda Appeal in Chile, Background Information for Editors, " 3 December 1971.

---

*I have calculated the per pound surplus as equal to 25 cents, that is, the spread between the price of copper received by Chile in 1971 (49 cents) and the estimated average unit cost of 24 cents. A metric ton is equal to 2, 204. 6 pounds.

13. The Chilean government announced it would not pay a $5.8 million debt installment to the Anaconda Co., The Times of the Americas, 28 June 1972, p. 11.

14. "From Riches to Rags," Forbes, 15 January 1972, p. 24.

15. "An Ex-banker Treats Copper's Sickest Giant," Business Week, 18 February 1972, p. 53.

16. Overseas Private Investment Corporation Annual Report Fiscal 1971, Washington, D.C., p. 34.

17. Ibid.

18. Anaconda Co., "Third Quarter Report 1971."

19. Topics, Overseas Private Investment Corp. 2, no. 1 (January 1973): 2.

20. Business Week, op. cit., p. 54.

21. New York Times, 25 January 1971, p. 19.

22. For the 1920s estimates, see C.W. Reynolds, "Chile and Copper," in M. Mamalakis and C.W. Reynolds, Essays on the Chilean Economy (New Haven: Yale University Economic Growth Center, 1965), pp. 365-79. For 1960-70, see Table 4.1.

23. Joseph Grunwald and Philip Musgrove, Natural Resources in Latin American Development (Baltimore and London: Johns Hopkins Press, 1970), p. 173.

24. Information provided to the author by the Anaconda Co. based on official statistics of its subsidiaries in Chile.

25. Derived from Kennecott Copper Corporation, Expropriation of the El Teniente Copper Mine by the Chilean Government, 1971, p. 2.

26. Thomas G. Sanders, Chile and its Copper, American Universities Field Staff, West Coast South American Series 16, no. 1, (March 1969): 4.

27. "Chuquicamata," Chile Exploration Co. (Anaconda), undated brochure.

28. Kennecott Copper Corporation, Expropriation of El Teniente Copper Mines by the Chilean Government, 1971, p. 4.

29. Paul Rosenstein-Rodan, "Multinational Investment in the Framework of Latin American Integration," Multinational Investment in the Economic Development and Integration of Latin America (Washington, D.C.: Inter-American Development Bank, 1968), p. 25.

30. Kennecott Copper Corporation, Expropriation of El Teniente, the World's Largest Underground Copper Mine, 1971, p. 15.

31. CORFO, Economic Notes, no. 21 (15 April 1968) and no. 61 (13 June 1970).

32. CORFO, op. cit., no. 21.

33. Kennecott Copper Corporation, Expropriation of the El Teniente Copper Mine by the Chilean Government, 1971, p. 6.

34. Information received by the author from the Anaconda Co. derived from official statistics of its Chilean subsidiaries.

35. Grunwald and Musgrove, op. cit., p. 72.

36. Oficina de Planificacion Nacional, <u>Antecedentes Sobre</u> el Desarollo Chileno 1960-70, serie no. 1, (ODEPLAN), Planes Sexenales (Santiago, Chile: Gobierno de Chile, 1971), p. 139, tables 96 and 97.

37. Kennecott Copper Corporation, <u>Expropriation of the El Teniente Copper Mine by the Chilean Government</u>, 1971, p. 1.

38. Oficina de la Planificacion Nacional, op. cit., p. 139.

39. <u>The Times of the Americas</u>, 19 January 1972, p. 1.

40. Norman Gall, <u>Copper is the Wage of Chile</u>, American Universities Field Staff, South American Series, 16, no. 3 (April 1972), p. 7.

41. Ibid., p. 6.

42. CORFO, <u>Chile Economic Notes</u>, 11, no. 33 (1 January 1973), p. 5.

43. "Calculating the Cost of Copper," <u>The Times of Zambia</u>, Lusaka, 28 July 1972, p. 8.

44. "How Politicians Manage Mines," <u>Business Week</u>, 21 August 1972, p. 33.

45. Gall, op. cit., p. 11.

46. Paul E. Sigmund, "The 'Invisible Blockade' and the Over-throw of Allende," <u>Foreign Affairs</u> 52, no. 2 (January 1974): 340.

47. <u>Wall Street Journal</u>, 30 September 1971, p. 7.

48. Statement by Alfonso Inestroza, president of the Central Bank of Chile, at the annual meeting of the International Monetary Fund and the International Bank for Reconstruction and Development, reproduced in CORFO, <u>Chile Economic News</u> 7, no. 30 (1 November 1972).

49. <u>Policies and Operation: The World Bank, IDA and IFC</u> (Washington, D.C.: International Bank for Reconstruction and Development, June 1971), p. 31.

50. Ibid.

6

LEGAL DIMENSIONS AND
ECONOMIC SANCTIONS

In both Cuba and Chile capital losses from expropriation suffered by U. S. nationals were on a grand scale and covered a spectrum of economic activities. This chapter estimates the value of assets taken in Cuba and Chile, examines the presumed legal basis for expropriatory acts, and compares the nature and impact of U. S. economic sanctions applied to both countries.

VALUES OF ASSETS TAKEN AND
SECTOR COMPOSITION

From 1959 the government of Cuba seized properties belonging to U. S. nationals with an estimated value of $1.8 billion (see Table 6.1). This magnitude is greater than the total amount expropriated by all other Communist countries combined, including the Soviet Union, Poland, Rumania, Czechoslovakia, Hungary, Yugoslavia, and Bulgaria. [1]

More than 8,800 claims were filed by U. S. nationals against Cuba under the Cuban Claims Program. The program was authorized as part of the work of the Foreign Claims Settlement Commission (FCSC), under Public Law 88-666, signed into law by President Lyndon Johnson on 16 October 1964. Terminated on 6 July 1972, the Cuban Claims Program was intended to provide for an orderly cataloging of claims, and to be a forum wherein claimants would be able to adduce evidence and receive an acknowledgement from their own government that they had, in fact, been the victim of unfair seizure. The very desirable and practical result in allowing a presettlement adjudication is that all such claims were investigated thoroughly and determined, "while witnesses' memories, and records are still

TABLE 6.1

Uncompensated Expropriation of U.S. Properties
in Cuba and Chile

Cuba (1959-60)	
Corporations	$1,578,500,000
Individuals	221,000,000
Total	$1,799,500,000
Chile (1971-73)	
Copper mining companies	$ 546,700,000-623,300,000
Other corporations	210,000,000
Total	$ 756,700,000-833,300,000

Sources: For Cuba, 1972 Foreign Claims Settlement Commission Annual Report (Washington, D.C.: Government Printing Office, 1973), p. 412, exhibit 15. For the Chilean copper mining companies, see "Gross company interests," Table 5.4 in this book. For other Chilean corporations, see U.S. Congress, House of Representatives, Committee on Foreign Affairs, United States-Chilean Relations, Hearings before the subcommittee on Inter-American Affairs, 93rd Cong., 1st sess., 6 March 1973, p. 7.

available and reliable."[2] The commission received and processed a total of 8,816 claims for an asserted value of $3,346 million. In its final report, the FCSC summed up its Cuban work by certifying 5,911 awards corresponding to $1.8 billion and denying 1195 claims for an asserted value of $1,547 million.[3] Of this sum, nearly $1.6 billion represents the certified claims of corporations; the value of properties taken from individuals is estimated at $221 million. To date, the Cuban revolutionary government has made no effort to indemnify Americans for properties seized.

The estimated value of U.S. investments taken in Chile by the government of the late President Salvador Allende falls between $747 million and $833 million. Of the total, the assets of the U.S. copper mining companies range between $537 million and $623 million, including notes repudiated by the Marxist coalition government. The remaining $210 million represents the equity investment of U. S. firms intervened or requisitioned by Chile and for which no compensation was forthcoming.

Unlike the U. S. investor experience in Cuba, an important number of American firms in Chile escaped the fate of uncompensated expropriation. The book value of equity investment purchased by the Chilean government is estimated at $70 million. [4] Most prominent among the companies bought out under Allende were Anglo Lautaro Nitrate, Armco Steel, Bethlehem Steel, Bank of America, the First National City Bank of New York, General Motors, Ralston Purina, and RCA. Also, throughout the three-year life of the Marxist regime, about 50 U. S. subsidiaries, with an estimated equity of $40-50 million, remained in private hands.

The U. S. government investment insurance program, managed by the Overseas Private Investment Corporation (OPIC), was available to U. S. investors in both Cuba and Chile. A share of the $600 million of new investments in Chile's large copper mines was insured against expropriation by the U. S. government. The investment insurance program did not become available in Cuba until 29 November 1957, about a year before Castro's takeover of the island. The program was not authorized for existing investments, and no contracts were issued on new commitments by U. S. firms in Cuba. The shift of a part of the expropriation risk in Chile to OPIC makes the U. S. government a direct claimant against the Chilean state.

U. S. direct investments in Cuba and Chile showed both similarities and differences in their sector composition prior to expropriation.[5] Export-oriented extractive industries and public utilities together commanded well over one-half of the U. S. business stake in the two countries. In Cuba, U. S. holdings for export were concentrated in sugar and in Chile copper mining was the dominant American-owned export industry. In 1970 copper, nitrate, and iron mining enterprises in Chile comprised over 60 percent of U. S. direct investments. Sugar estates and mills, together with nickel mining, accounted for about 30 percent of U. S. investments in Cuba in 1959. Public utilities comprised one-third of total U. S. holdings in Cuba and an estimated one-fourth in Chile. In both nations the share of general manufacturing in total U. S. accumulated investment was modest (12 percent in Cuba, 9 percent in Chile). However, the inclusion of petroleum refining would raise the participation of manufacturing in U. S. investments in Cuba to 27 percent, or slightly above the share of sugar operations in the total. Commerce and hotels, though qualitatively important, absorbed only from 5-7 percent of the U. S. direct investments in Cuba and Chile on the eve of their expropriation.

Table 6.2 lists the ten U. S. companies with the highest losses incurred in Cuba. Their combined assets exceed $1 billion, or 65 percent of the losses suffered by all U. S. corporate subsidiaries in Cuba. Extremely high capital losses were sustained by two public utility enterprises: the Cuban Electric Company (a subsidiary of the American and Foreign Power Co.), $268 million; and ITT, $131 million. Five of the companies on the list were predominantly in sugar growing and milling, and two were engaged in petroleum refining for the domestic market. The Moa Bay Mining Company (a subsidiary of Freeport Sulphur) was involved in the mining and refining of nickel.

TABLE 6.2

Ten Highest Certifications of Loss Under
the Cuban Claims Program

Claimant	Amount of Award
Cuban Electric Co.	$ 267,568,414
ITT	130,679,758
West India Co.	108,975,068
Moa Bay Mining Co.	88,349,000
United Fruit Sugar Co.	85,110,147
West Indies Sugar Co.	84,880,958
American Sugar Co.	81,011,240
Standard Oil Co.	71,611,003
Bangor Punta Corp.	53,081,110
Texaco, Inc.	50,081,110
Total	$1,021,645,816

Source: 1972 Foreign Claims Settlement Commission Annual Report (Washington, D. C.: Government Printing Office, 1973) p. 414.

LEGALITY OF EXPROPRIATORY ACTIONS

In June 1960, Premier Castro declared, "We'll take and take until not even the nails of their shoes are left. We will take American investments penny by penny until nothing is left."[6] By the close of 1960 virtually all U. S.-owned properties on the island had been confiscated by the Cuban state.

The presumed legal basis for the taking of U. S. properties in Cuba was contained in three decree laws: the Agrarian Reform Law of 3 June 1959, the Law of Nationalization of 6 July 1960, and Law 890 of 14 October 1960. (See Appendix B for the list of U. S. properties expropriated or intervened by the Cuban government.) Ranches and sugar cane lands belonging to U. S. owners were expropriated under the provisions of the Agrarian Reform Law. The overwhelming number of U. S. holdings, including public utilities, sugar mills, factories, banks, and insurance companies, were taken under the so-called Law of Nationalization.

A provision for compensation in 30-year bonds at two percent interest was contained in the nationalization law. However, this provision was linked to the creation of a special fund to which contributions would come from the sale of sugar to the U. S. market--but only <u>after</u> Cuban sales exceeded 3.5 million tons annually at a minimum price of 5.75 cents per pound.[7] Compensation, in other words, would not become effective unless the then prevailing sugar quota of 3.2 million tons and the U. S. price of sugar were both raised.[8] "The practical effect of this provision," as Lynn Bender makes clear, "was the effective non-payment of all nationalized properties, for such was contingent upon attainment of sales to the U. S. market at volume and price levels far in excess of those prevailing at the time."[9]

The seizures of U. S. corporate investments and properties of individual U. S. citizens by the Castro regime did not conform to domestic law. Article 24 of the Cuban constitution of 1940 guaranteed the protection of property on a nondiscriminatory basis and established the juridical procedure for special cases involving expropriation. Property could be expropriated only for just cause involving a public utility or social interest, and then only through prior indemnification of the owner in cash as determined by the courts.[10]

In Chile, the nationalization of U. S. copper mining investments gives, on first reflection, the appearance of a concern for legal scruples. The measure was carried out through a constitutional amendment approved by the Chilean Congress. However, the expropriation bill, signed into law on 16 July 1971, as interpreted by President Allende, specifically denied the large U. S. copper mining companies the right of recourse through the regular courts of law to the Chilean Supreme Court. The amendment, as noted in the previous chapter, authorized the president to make a series of deducations from the value of compensation including alleged "excess profits" earned by the U. S. companies between 1955-70. (This provision, however, was permissive rather than obligatory.) As noted before, Allende set the amount of "excess profits" that would be deducted from compensation to be paid to U. S. copper mining companies at $774 million--according to his calculations, profits allegedly received over 12 percent of book value from 5 May 1955 (the date of the "New

Deal" law) and 31 December 1970. On this accounting, Kennecott had earned "excess profits" of $410 million and Anaconda, $364 million. This deduction alone was to transform the U. S. copper mining companies from creditors to debtors.

The deduction of "excess profits" became the center of the conflict between the Chilean state and the U. S. companies. Both Anaconda and Kennecott filed appeal briefs with the Special Copper Tribunal seeking compensation for properties taken by the Chilean government. In August 1972 the tribunal denied the petitions of the U. S. companies for reconsideration of the deduction of alleged "excess profits" from any compensation paid them for their expropriated assets because of "the absolute incompetence of the Court to know such matters."[11] In reporting on the appeal process in Chile, the respected and widely read Mexican financial journal Comercio Exterior de Mexico erroneously reported that,

> After nationalization of the copper industry by the
> Chilean government, July 1971, special courts in
> Chile arrived at the decision that Kennecott had
> obtained excess profits from its operations and was
> therefore not entitled to indemnization.[12]

However, as we have shown above, the special tribunal did not determine that the U. S. companies earned excess profits, declaring this question to be beyond its competence.

In an address before the American Bar Association National Institute, Carlos Fortin of the Chilean Copper Corporation (CODELCO) presented the Chilean government's case. He argued that the purpose of the "excess profits" provision was to introduce a historical rectification for a wrong done against the Chilean economy over a period of years. It was essentially an "act of revision of formulas that were legal at the time at which they were applied but which with the perspective of time appeared as unconscionable to the national interest . . ."[13] The legal basis for the deduction of excess profits is not the illegality of the acts,* according to Fortin, but the

---

*Novoa Monreal, in his comprehensive treatise La Nacionalizacion del Cobre, argues that the deduction of excess profits retroactively would have been impossible in accordance with existing legal principles. It was therefore necessary to give priority to "reasons of social justice and close the road to possible judicial claims for compensation on the part of the companies." Eduardo Novoa Monreal, La Nacionalizacion del Cobre: Comentarios y Documentos (Santiago: Empresa Editora Nacional Quimantu, 1972), p. 155 (author's translation).

contention that there was an unjust enrichment for the companies deriving from those acts.

In their briefs before the Special Copper Tribunal, the U.S. companies held that reference had been made in the Chilean Chamber of Deputies concerning the right of review of the "excess profits" and also that the comptroller general, in his memorandum to the president, expressed his opinion that the "excess profits" could be reviewed by the special tribunal.

Significantly, Enrique Urrutia, president of the Special Copper Tribunal, who served concurrently as president of the Supreme Court of Chile, disagreed with the tribunal's decision. In his dissenting opinion, Urrutia noted that Resolution 1803 (XVII), approved by the General Assembly of the United Nations in 1962, served as the primary and justifying basis for effecting the expropriation of the copper companies, and that, in effect, that resolution, together with recognizing the inalienable right of every state to freely dispose of its wealth and its natural resources in conformity with its national interests and the respect for the economic independence of the states, established also that in cases of nationalization "the owner shall be paid appropriate compensation, in accordance with the rules in force in the State taking such measures in the exercise of its sovereignty and in accordance with International Law."[14] In any case in which the question of compensation gives origin to litigation, the national jurisdiction of the state adopting such measures must be exhausted. Further,

> That, on the basis of the Resolution of the United Nations cited above and the other reasons that have been expounded, the creation of this Tribunal would have been merely illusory if it were to hear only the protest against the fixed indemnizations, if at the same time the affected parties were denied the right to protest against the decision on excessive profits before the Tribunal, a decision reached without the affected parties being heard and under circumstances by which the Constituent Assembly considered them as forming part of a single process, as was recognized also by the Comptroller General of the Republic in his resolution No. 529 of October 11, 1971 when he stated that: "the process of the determination of the indemnization corresponding to the expropriated companies" includes three perfectly defined phases as follows: (a) accounting phase; (b) basis of specific deductions; and (c) "phase of the deduction of excessive profits" [emphasis added].[15]

It is ironic that U. S. policy under the John F. Kennedy and Lyndon Johnson administrations helped pave the way toward uncompensated expropriation of American-owned assets in Chile. To obtain Alliance for Progress financial assistance, President Jorge Allesandri was compelled to modify the Chilean constitution in 1963 to permit deferred payment for expropriated agricultural properties. Before the passage of this partial amendment and the 1967 Agrarian Reform Law, Chilean citizens could not be deprived of their property without prior compensation in cash.

Equally significant for an understanding of the subsequent copper dispute was the change that occurred in the process for judicial review involving agrarian reform. The implications of the 1967 Agrarian Reform Law are trenchantly analyzed by Alamiro Avila Martel, professor of legal history at the University of Chile. He states that the 1967 amendment to article 10 of the constitution reflects in many respects a conscious determination to reverse the law that had developed in Chile as a result of the constitutional texts, the decisions of the Chilean Supreme Court, and the writings of the leading commentators.[16] He shows that, for practical purposes, the Chilean agrarian reform after 1967 became insulated from normal judicial procedures; and the definition of "social function" of property was expanded as far as to contain no practical limits. Writing before the passage of the Copper Expropriation Bill, Avila Martel concludes his essay with a portentous sentence, "But the Constitutional shields for the individual against the State have, in the area of property, all but disappeared."[17]

On 7 September 1972 the Kennecott Copper Corp. announced that, "because of the Chilean government's determination in violation of international law that no compensation will be paid for the expropriated properties, it is withdrawing from further legal proceedings in Chile and will pursue in other nations its remedies for the confiscated assets."[18] At the same time, Kennecott notified all customers of the El Teniente mine of its rights of ownership in El Teniente copper and its proceeds. By the spring of 1973 court actions initiated by Kennecott were pending in France, Holland, Germany, and Italy in which the company has requested the impoundment of copper shipments coming from its former El Teniente mine in Chile. Kennecott's legal efforts to pursue its "other nation's remedies," along with ITT's attempts to meddle in Chilean politics, were characterized by President Allende as "aggression of transnational corporations in Chile."[19]

The legality of taking U. S. investments in enterprises other than the copper companies is also questionable. A law that remained on the books but long had been forgotten was revived by the Marxist government to justify state intervention or requisition of private firms, including U. S.-owned enterprises. Back in 1932, the short-lived

Socialist Republic, struggling to cope with a depression, decreed
that the national government temporarily could take over any company
that failed to supply vital products because of labor or financial problems. Under Allende (with the Communists or Socialists in control
of most labor unions) labor disputes and factory seizures became
occasions for permanent state intervention. The courts ruled that the
firms should revert to their owners after they resumed normal
operations, but the administration simply ignored the decisions. [20]

At the time of the military coup in September 1973, some 500
enterprises had come under government control. Fewer than 100 of
these actions had received congressional approval. Consequently,
more than 400 of these enterprises were nationalized, intervened, or
occupied by the workers with the Marxist government's acquiescence.
In about 40 such cases, U. S. capital was involved. On 23 August
1973, the Chilean Congress passed a resolution accusing the administration of "grave breaches of constitutional and legal order. " The
resolution cited the Allende regime for disregarding repeatedly
decisions of congress, the supreme court, the comptroller general,
and the constitutional tribunal; for encouragement of illegal occupations of farms and industries; for arming and training of para-military
groups; and for instigation of subversion within the armed forces. [21]

U. S. SANCTIONS AND THE CUBAN ECONOMY

The ouster by Fidel Castro of his first president, Manuel
Urrutia, a political moderate, proved to be a turning point in the
Cuban revolution. Osvaldo Dorticos, a revolutionary theorist, succeeded to the presidency; and men such as Ernesto "Che" Guevara
and Raul Castro gained in power. Guevara's appointment during
November 1959 as president of the National Bank of Cuba portended
a significant change in the island's economic relations with the United
States. Shortly after his appointment to this key post, payments to
the American and British oil companies that supplied Cuba with
petroleum were stopped. The Cuban government decided to import
crude oil from the Soviet Union to take the place of the fuel supplied
by Western companies through their Venezuelan subsidiaries. The
companies, whose claim on the Cuban government for crude petroleum
imports had risen to approximately $80 million, refused to refine oil
supplied by the USSR. The Cuban government then proceeded to seize
these refineries without offering indemnity. Also, during the autumn
of 1959 the Dorticos government seized farms and ranches with all
their improvements and chattels--without offering compensation to
their owners.

The U. S. government, recognizing Cuba's right to expropriate
foreign-owned properties provided that prompt, just, and effective

compensation be given, sought from early 1959 until mid-1960 to negotiate differences. Dwight D. Eisenhower's administration offered Cuba economic assistance* during Premier Fidel Castro's visit to the United States in April 1959; and in January 1960 declared its willingness to negotiate all disputes, including those arising from Cuban seizure of American properties.[22] In both instances there was no official response from Cuba. As Theodore Draper observed, "Only the ingenuous can still believe that Fidel Castro walked into a Communist trap or that he gave up the democratic road because the United States did not give him enough support in his early months in power."[23]

In mid-July 1960, following the confiscation of most U. S. business holdings in Cuba, the U. S. Congress reduced the island's sugar quota and set it at zero for 1961 and the following years.[24] Cuba's share in the domestic market was reallocated mainly to other countries already having quotas to the extent that those countries were expected to have supplies available. Further, the elimination of the sugar quota was followed in October 1960 by an embargo on U. S. exports to Cuba, covering everything except medical supplies and foodstuffs. It was not until three years after the cutoff of the Cuban sugar quota, on 8 July 1963, that Cuban property in the United States was blocked.[25]

Cuba's signing of a Trade and Payments Agreement with the USSR on 13 February 1960 was followed shortly by similar bilateral agreements with other Communist nations. The revolutionary government declined to participate in the newly formed Inter-American Development Bank, and in late 1960 Cuba withdrew its representation from the World Bank. Cuba became the first Marxist-Leninist nation in the Western Hemisphere, as acknowledged by Premier Castro in his 2 December 1961 nationwide address. In identifying himself as a Marxist-Leninist, Castro explained that he had concealed his Communist beliefs from Cubans and from American friends for years "because otherwise we might have alienated the bourgeoisie and other

---

*Assistant Secretary of State for Latin American Affairs, Roy Rubottom, "invited Castro's aides to discuss Cuba's financial needs and offered help." See Robert F. Smith, The United States and Cuba: Business and Diplomacy, 1917-1960 (New York: Bookman Associates, 1962), pp. 157-159. During his trip to the United States in April 1959, Premier Castro forbade the financial experts who accompanied him to engage in talks or negotiations regarding U. S. assistance to Cuba. This has been confirmed by Rufo Lopez-Fresquet in an oral statement to the author. Lopez-Fresquet, currently professor of economics at the University of the Pacific, served as Cuba's minister of finance from 1959-70.

forces which we knew we would eventually have to fight."[26] With the takeover of 55,000 small private businesses in the spring of 1968, the Cuban state completed the socialization of the economy.*

In January 1962 Cuba was suspended from the Organization of American States (OAS), which also recommended the imposition of economic sanctions in retaliation for Cuba's subversive activities in the Western Hemisphere. The OAS position hardened in 1964 when, after a formal Venezuelan complaint against a Cuban-sponsored guerrilla invasion, every OAS government except Mexico severed its trade and diplomatic ties to Havana.

Cuba's radical reorientation toward the Soviet bloc since 1960 has diminished its international economic options. The island's economy accumulated a large external debt, exhausted its foreign exchange reserves, and has become firmly tied to the centrally planned nations, mainly the Soviet Union, through barter arrangements and economic and military aid.[27] From a purely economic point of view, the trade relationship with the USSR, whose ports are more than 5,000 miles away, is an unnatural one.

The U.S. embargo of Cuba, according to Donald Losman's comprehensive study, has been very damaging to the island's economic development.[28] Before the revolution, Cuba's capital equipment came almost wholly from the United States, as did the bulk of its raw materials. This imported machinery and equipment employed in the island's agricultural, industrial, transport, power, and communications sectors embodied a specific technological system. After the rupture in trade relations between the United States and Cuba, the Soviet bloc suppliers were unable to serve adequately Cuba's existing capital stock: there existed a lack of complementarity between Cuba's import needs and the bloc's export capabilities. Indeed, Cuban officials were shocked to discover that the USSR and the other East European socialist countries were far behind the United States in technology. Thus, according to Losman, the embargo of replacement parts had the same effect as "pinpoint bombing or industrial sabotage--capital equipment has been rendered economically useless (although physically

---

*In May 1968 the "Committees for the Defense of the Revolution" (CDR) took over and nationalized 55,000 small private businesses, grocery stores, repair shops, artisan establishments, and such. This action was called "tearing capitalism out by the roots" and furthered Fidel Castro's long cherished objective: to make Cuba the first truly Communist country in the world. Fenton Wheeler, "Fidel Castro Launching Cuba on Revolutionary Offensive," Morning Advocate (Baton Rouge, La.), May 16, 1968, p. 3-D.

intact)."[29] Considering the massive economic assistance provided to Cuba by the Soviet bloc, mainly the USSR, a significant share of the embargo's incidence has been shifted from the Cuban economy to the Soviet Union.

The structural changes that have taken place in Cuba's foreign trade involve primarily the direction of commodity flows rather than their composition. In a brief span of four years, from 1960, Cuba's trade with the United States, its predominant and traditional trading partner, virtually ceased. The Soviet Union and other Communist nations have since 1962 accounted for about 80 percent of Cuba's trade turnover--a dramatic example of geographic trade diversion.

Cuba's external payments position since 1960 has been characterized by a widening trade gap, the consequence of stagnation in export values, and a protracted rise in commodity imports. The associated explosive growth in external public debt during the 1960s has not been matched by improvement in debt-service capacity, for both total production (GNP) and exports have failed to expand. Eleven years after the revolution, Cuba's cumulative sugar deficit with the Soviet Union exceeded 10 million tons; and, by the end of 1970, Cuba's cumulative trade deficit with the USSR had reached an estimated $2.2 billion. Cuba's total indebtedness to the Soviet Union, including interest on debt, hard currency assistance, and other economic assistance, was believed to be about $2.6 billion, with aid from other Communist countries adding another $300 million. Including payment of premium prices for Cuban sugar, totaling about $1 billion from 1961, Soviet economic assistance to Cuba (excluding grant military assistance) thus averaged about $370 million annually for the decade, or more than $1 million per day.[30]

The revolutionary government's efforts to introduce a crash program of industrialization in a period of multiplying shortages of both trained personnel and foreign exchange during the early 1960s proved abortive. Following severe reductions in the island's sugar crop, Primier Castro announced in late 1963 that Cuba would leave behind the "stage of ignorance" and henceforth concentrate on what it could do best: grow sugar. Though important advances have been made in the development of Cuba's merchant marine and fishing industry since 1960, the island's dependency on sugar exports as a source of income and foreign exchange has not diminished in comparison with the 1950s.

The island's real per capita GNP, according to the World Bank, declined at an average annual rate of 1.2 percent during 1960-71 period.[31] A State Department estimate indicates that Cuba's per capita GNP (in constant 1957 prices) declined from $428 in 1958, the year prior to the revolution, to $388 in 1970.[32] The island's shrinking per capita income was associated with a growing shortage of

consumer goods and comprehensive rationing. In the now famous
26 July 1970 speech, Premier Castro provided his audience with an
itemized inventory of the revolution's economic failures. Cuba's
economic problems, as Robert F. Smith makes clear, arose out of
the interrelated combination of such factors as bad planning, doctri-
naire utopianism, administrative inexperience, insufficiency of
trained manpower, several years of drought, the hurricanes of 1963
and 1964, and U. S. economic sanctions that resulted in the almost
complete disruption of traditional patterns of trade. [33] With the
passing of time, Cuba's capital stock progressively is being reoriented
to Soviet bloc and to a lesser degree Western European equipment
specifications; but the island's massive loss of "human capital"--the
exiled managers, professionals, technicians, and skilled workers--
is not repaired as easily.

Cuba's fundamental political and economic reorientation
since 1960 has also cut the nation off from other economic stimuli.
The transfer of advanced U. S. managerial and technical knowledge
through U. S. subsidiaries operating in Cuba ceased with the confiscation of U. S. business assets. Also, the island lost the opportunity
to participate as principal beneficiary in the Caribbean tourist boom
of the 1960s. Without doubt, Cuba would have captured the lion's
share of the U. S. tourist dollar; instead, Puerto Rico, Jamaica, and
the lesser Caribbean islands gained much of the tourist income that
would otherwise have been Cuba's.

Cuba became tied even more closely to the USSR following
Castro's visit to Moscow in connection with the celebration of the 50th
anniversary of the Russian Revolution. The five economic cooperation
agreements signed by Premier Castro and Secretary Leonid Brezhnev
on 23 December 1972 in effect wrote off Cuba's huge accumulated debt
to the Soviet Union, extended long-term economic development credits,
and doubled the price of Cuba's two basic exports to the USSR: sugar
and nickel. [34] The development credits will permit the rebuilding of
Cuba's nickel and cobalt plants and seven sugar mills. The corollary
of this massive injection of Soviet aid into the economy is likely to be
Cuban ideological conformity and increasing Russian supervision of
the island's economic life.

Since the restoration of official ties between Chile's former
Marxist coalition government and Cuba in November 1970, there has
been a growing trend towards ending the Castro regime's isolation
in the Americas. Chile's example has been followed by the military
junta in Peru, by the four small English-speaking states in the
Caribbean (Jamaica, Barbados, Trinidad-Tobago, and Guiana), and
by the latest Peronist regime in Argentina.

In his 1971 report to Congress on U. S. foreign policy, President Richard Nixon stated, "Cuba continued to exclude itself from the

inter-American system by its encouragement and support of revolution and its military ties to the Soviet Union. The latter meanwhile attempted to expand its influence and its military presence."[35] The main obstacle to rapprochement between the United States and Cuba, in the view of the Republican administration, is the Castro government's military ties to the USSR and its long range revolutionary goals in the Americas.

A number of articles and memoranda have appeared recently that favor "normalization" of U.S.-Cuban relations.[36] Normalization would presumably involve the resumption of diplomatic relations and abandonment of the U.S. policy of economic denial. The Congressional Conference on U.S.-Cuba Relations, held in the Senate on 19-20 April 1972, reached a consensus on how the freeze on U.S.-Cuban relations could be "constructively altered." The conference, an activity of the Fund for New Priorities, a New York based organization "concerned with public issues, social justice, and international accord," was sponsored by 29 senators and representatives, including two Republicans. The participants proposed, among several measures, (1) the removal of the trade embargo, (2) the extension of long-term agricultural credits to Cuba, and (3) that a reasonable rent should be paid for leasing the facilities at Guantanamo or, alternatively, the U.S. naval base should be returned to Cuba. No proposals were forthcoming concerning the fate of Cuba's estimated 70,000-90,000 political prisoners,* and the legitimate property claims of U.S. citizens against Cuba were treated as a matter of little weight in the conciliation effort.

In the spring of 1974, responding to pressure from the new Peron regime, the United States was prepared to relax its economic sanctions against Cuba. The Argentine government wished to export 42,000 cars and trucks from three American subsidiaries to Cuba as part of a $1.2 billion trade agreement. U.S. authorization for the Argentine subsidiaries of Ford, General Motors, and Chrysler to ship approximately $75 million of vehicles to Cuba virtually was assured by June 1974. The Senate Foreign Relations Committee approved the proposal, and it was expected to be passed by the full Senate and possibly by the House. The agreement was part of the overall plan devised by Secretary of State Henry Kissinger at the 1974 meeting of the Organization of American States, implementing his pledge to do his utmost to have the U.S. remove restrictions on trade with Latin America. Under the American Export Control Act, the trade embargo

---

*In 1971 the Inter-American Human Rights Commission placed the number of political prisoners on the Communist island at between 70,000 and 90,000. See The Times of the Americas, July 12, 1972, p. 6.

of Cuba applies to U. S. corporations and their overseas subsidiaries. The State Department has called the granting of the export licenses an "exception" and has insisted that there has been no change in the U. S. policy of economic isolation of Cuba. *

THE U. S. RESPONSE TO THE CHILEAN EXPROPRIATION

During the early months of President Allende's administration the U. S. government exercised restraint in its relations with Chile. President Nixon tried to avoid a confrontation with Chile despite the Marxist orientation of her new regime, and emphasized that the U. S. is prepared "to have the kind of relationship with the Chilean government that it is prepared to have with us."[37]

Notwithstanding President Allende's position that retroactive "excess profits" would be deducted from the final settlement with U. S. copper firms, there remained some prospect for negotiation. A few days after Allende's announcement, Chile's foreign minister, Clodomiro Almeyda, met in Washington with Presidential Adviser Kissinger. Almeyda told Kissinger that Chile was willing to negotiate the $774 million "excess profits" figure, and the meeting ended with mutual assurances that the copper issue would not jeopardize the long-term U. S.-Chile relations.[38] Chile's Ambassador to the United States, Orlando Letelier, also suggested that the $774 million figure probably would come down in the final reckoning.

Washington's momentary optimism was dashed, however, by the announcement on 11 October 1971 that Chile's comptroller general had found Anaconda and Kennecott liable for the full $774 million in "excess profits"; and that the companies would not receive compensation. Referring to the comptroller general's ruling, U. S. Secretary of State William P. Rogers issued the following statement on the Chilean nationalizations,

---

*American directors of subsidiaries that violate the act are liable to penalties of 10 years in prison and a $10,000 fine. In defense of the administration's position, it should be noted that foreign subsidiaries operating in the United States are required to obey U. S. laws; therefore, U. S. subsidiaries operating abroad hardly can invoke immunity from the laws of host nations. Further, the prices charged Cuba by Chrysler, GM, and Ford in Argentina are undoubtedly substantially higher than if the autos and trucks were exported from the U. S. parent companies. These higher Argentine prices reflect extremely high average effective rates of protection for manufactured goods in that nation.

The United States Government is deeply disap-
pointed and disturbed at this serious departure
from accepted standards of international law.
Under established principles of international law,
the expropriation must be accompanied by reasonable provision for payment of just compensation.
The United States has made clear to the Government
of Chile its hope that a solution could be found on a
reasonable and pragmatic basis consistent with
international law. [39]

On 19 January 1972, President Nixon issued a stern warning
aimed at nations such as Chile that expropriate U. S. investments
without paying "prompt, adequate, and effective compensation." The
policy statement, "Economic Assistance and Investment Security in
Developing Nations," served notice that when a country expropriates
a significant U. S. interest without making reasonable provision for
just compensation to U. S. citizens, the United States (1) will not
extend new bilateral economic benefits to the expropriating country
and (2) will withhold its support from loans under consideration in
multinational development banks. [40]
    The new policy of economic sanctions was the culmination of
a lengthy debate within the Nixon administration that began shortly
after the Republican president assumed office. Complicating the
framing of the policy on investment security was a division between
the Treasury and State Departments over how hard a line the administration should take. The State Department sought to maintain a
posture of maximum flexibility, and the Treasury Department
(especially under former Secretary John Connally) took a tougher,
more nationalistic line. The policy debate concerning the proper U. S.
response must be viewed against the background of significant events:
the Peruvian junta's intractable position regarding compensation of
the International Petroleum Corporation, major expropriations of
U. S. investments in Bolivia and Chile, and the growing impatience of
the House of Representatives with the administration's "soft line."
Within a few weeks of the President's policy statement, Congress
enacted the Gonzalez Amendment instructing U. S. representatives in
multinational lendings institutions to vote against countries expropriating U. S. investments without compensation.
    The position of the United States now became clear: the
Republican administration would press for a compensation link in the
context of the Chilean debt renegotiation. In November 1971 President Allende declared a moratorium on the lion's share of Chile's
external public debt; and in January 1972, two months after the
suspension of debt service, the Chilean government entered into

critical negotiations with her international creditors, including the United States, to reschedule payments on a major portion of her foreign debt. * Allende's government, the U. S. delegates noted, had failed to compensate the U. S. -owned copper companies for the equities taken by Chile and had repudiated debts previously guaranteed by the Chilean government arising out of partial nationalization of the properties. The United States would not agree to help ease Chile's debt burden unless compensation on these matters were to be forthcoming. Fortunately for the United States, the European creditors in the Paris Club were tough-minded about collecting debts; they supported the U. S. position on compensation.

On 19 April in Paris the participants announced the successful outcome of the multinational debt renegotiation meetings. [41] The Chilean officials agreed to recognize and pay all foreign debts and also accepted "the principle of payment of just compensation for all nationalizations in accordance with Chilean and international law. " Chile also agreed to send regular reports on its balance of payments to its creditors through the International Monetary Fund. In exchange for these concessions, representatives of the creditor countries agreed that, in view of Chile's balance of payments situation, they would recommend to their governments the refinancing of 70 percent of the interest and amortization due between November 1971 (when Chile had placed a moratorium on most external debt payments) and December 1972. Service payments falling due in this period would be rescheduled over a six-year period, following two years of grace.

---

*In the course of the first four months of 1972 the Chilean delegation met with representatives of the Paris Club, a group of 12 creditor nations including the United States, Canada, Japan, and European nations. The Chilean delegation requested a three-year moratorium on all outstanding debts owed the creditors. Chile's total external debt as of November 1970, according to Allende's administration, exceeded $3 billion, without including the $728 million owed by the nationalized copper companies. Annual service of this debt, about $400 million, would commit 35 percent of the nation's export proceeds. Approximately $1. 5 billion of Chile's outstanding debt was owed to U. S. creditors, including over $900 million to U. S. Government agencies such as the Export-Import Bank and the Overseas Private Investment Corporation (OPIC). Chile's precarious external financial situation was aggravated by the heavy depletion of its foreign exchange reserves between the time of President Allende's assumption of office and the autumn of 1971. CORFO, Chile Economic Notes, no. 89 (November 1971) and no. 91 (December 1971).

Negotiations for the refinancing of the Chilean debt for 1973-74 were resumed in December 1972, but in April 1973 the discussions between Chile and the United States were broken off with no agreement between the two parties. The U. S. delegation noted that there had been no effort made by the Chilean government to compensate the U. S. companies for their expropriated properties. Following the breakdown of the debt negotiations, John Crimmins, acting undersecretary of state for inter-American affairs, told a House of Representatives committee that the United States would not waive the question of compensation.

The U. S. response to uncompensated expropriation in Chile was both limited and less consequential than in the Cuban situation. Even if a trade embargo of Chile had been considered, the U. S. leverage against the South American nation, considering its geographically diversified trade pattern, would have been largely ineffective. By the end of 1971 the Export-Import Bank had suspended indefinitely all new committments to Chile. On the other hand, the Food for Peace Program distributed $10 million worth of food during Allende's three years in power from November 1970 to September 1973.[42] Other nations, according to official Chilean sources, provided substantial short- and long-term credits to Chile, including an estimated $550 million from the Soviet Union. What, then, was the effect of Washington's "invisible blockade" of Chile? Paul E. Sigmund in his definitive Foreign Affairs article concludes,

> . . . it thus appears that the principal result of the half-hearted American effort to put pressure on the Chileans to persuade them to come to terms with the copper companies was a considerable increase in alternative sources of loans and credit to Chile, which more than counterbalanced reductions from U. S. and U. S.-influenced sources.[43]

NOTES

1. Sidney Freidberg, "The Measure of Damages in Claims Against Cuba," Inter-American Economic Affairs 23, no. 1 (Summer 1969): 72. See also Edward D. Re, "The Foreign Claims Settlement Commission and the Cuban Claims Program," International Lawyer 1, no. 1 (October 1966).

2. U. S. Congress, House Committee on Foreign Affairs, Claims of U. S. Nationals Against the Government of Cuba, Hearings before the Sub-committee on Inter-American Affairs, 88th Cong., 2nd sess., 1964, p. 18.

3. 1972 Foreign Claims Settlement Commission Annual Report (Washington, D.C.: Government Printing Office, 1973), p. 412, exhibit 15.

4. U.S. Congress, House Committee on Foreign Affairs, United States-Chilean Relations, Hearings Before the Subcommittee on Inter-American Affairs, 93rd Cong., 1st sess., 1973, p. 7.

5. Survey of Current Business (September 1960): 20, table 1; and (November 1973): 30-31, table 7B.

6. New York Times, 21 August 1960, sec. 3F, p. 1.

7. Lynn Darrell Bender, "U.S. Claims Against the Cuban Government: An Obstacle to Rapprochement?" Inter-American Economic Affairs 27, no. 1 (Summer 1973): 4.

8. From 1955-59, the U.S. price averaged 5.2 cents a pound compared with the average world price of 3.7 cents. See International Monetary Fund, International Financial Statistics, various issues, 1955-59 (Washington, D.C.: International Monetary Fund).

9. Bender, op cit.

10. Cuban Economic Research Project, Un Estudio Sobre Cuba (Coral Gables: University of Miami Press, 1963), p. 1382.

11. CORFO, Chile Economic Notes, no. 3 (1 September 1972).

12. Comercio Exterior de Mexico 17, no. 11 (November 1972): 27.

13. Address given by Carlos Fortin, Representative of Corporation del Cobre in Chile in England, before the American Bar Association National Institute (reproduced in Chile Economic News 21, no. 43 (1 June 1974).

14. Dissenting opinion of Enrique Urrutia, president of the Special Copper Tribunal and president of the Supreme Court of the Republic of Chile, reproduced in Kennecott Copper Corp., Confiscation of El Teniente, Supplement No. 3 (December 1972), pp. 37-43.

15. Ibid., p. 42.

16. Alamiro Avila Martel, with Manuel Sabat Monguillot, "Chile," in Andreas F. Lowenfield, ed., Expropriation in the Americas: A Comparative Law Study (New York: Dunellen, 1971), p. 92.

17. Ibid., p. 109.

18. Kennecott Copper Corp., op. cit., p. i.

19. Speech delivered by Salvador Allende, president of the Republic of Chile, before the General Assembly of the United Nations, 4 December 1972, pp. 17-18.

20. Wall Street Journal, 24 October 1972, p. 1.

21. Latin American Report 2, no. 2 (September 1973): 3.

22. Arthur P. Whitaker and David C. Jordan, Nationalism in Contemporary Latin America (New York: Free Press, 1966), p. 156.

23. Theodore Draper, Castro's Revolution, Myths and Realities (New York: Praeger Publishers, 1962), p. 107.

24. U.S. Congress, House Committee on Agriculture, The United States Sugar Program, 91st Cong., 2nd sess., 1970, p. 38.

25. U.S. Congress, Hearings Before the Sub-committee on Inter-American Affairs, op. cit., p. 45.

26. Cuba, the U.S. and Russia, 1960-63 (New York: Facts on File, Inc., 1964), p. 55.

27. For an extended discussion of the 1960-70 decade, see my chapter "Cuba's International Economic Relations" in Carmelo Mesa-Lago, ed., Revolutionary Change in Cuba (Pittsburgh: University of Pittsburgh Press, 1971).

28. Donald L. Losman, "The Embargo of Cuba: An Economic Appraisal," paper delivered at the Southern Economic Association meeting, 9 November 1973. See also Losman, "International Economic Sanctions: The Boycotts of Cuba, Israel, and Rhodesia," University of Florida, Ph.D. dissertation, 1969, pp. 18-28, 41-53, and 85-93.

29. Ibid., p. 14.

30. Department of State, "Republic of Cuba," background notes, November 1971, p. 6.

31. World Bank Atlas: Population, per Capita Product and Growth Rates (Washington, D.C.: International Bank for Reconstruction and Development, 1973).

32. Department of State, op. cit., p. 4.

33. Robert F. Smith, "Castro's Revolution: Domestic Sources and Consequences," in John N. Plank, ed., Cuba and the United States: Long Range Perspectives (Washington: Brookings Institution, 1967), p. 65.

34. "Acuerdos economicos con la Union Sovietica," Comercio Exterior 23, no. 1 (January 1973): 38.

35. Department of State, op. cit., p. 7.

36. For example, Edward Gonzalez, "The United States and Castro: Breaking the Deadlock," Foreign Affairs 50, no. 4 (July 1972); and Jorge I. Dominguez, "Freeze or Thaw? The Pros and Cons of Recognizing Castro's Cuba," Harper's Magazine 246, no. 1475 (April 1973).

37. U.S. Congress, House Committee on Foreign Affairs, United States-Chilean Relations, Hearings Before the Subcommittee on Inter-American Affairs, 93rd Cong., 1st sess., 1973, p. 41.

38. Mark L. Chadwin, "Foreign Policy Report/Nixon Administration Debates New Position on Latin America," National Journal 4, no. 3 (15 January 1972): 10.

39. U.S. Department of State Release No. 234, 13 October 1971.

40. Office of the White House press secretary, policy statement, Economic Assistance and Investment Security in Developing Nations, 19 January 1972.

41. Paris Club, press release, Paris, 19 April 1972.

42. Paul E. Sigmund, "The 'Invisible Blockade' and the Overthrow of Allende," Foreign Affairs 52, no. 2 (January 1974): 334.

43. Ibid.

7

EXPROPRIATION IN
THREE COUNTRIES:
AN OVERVIEW

In the three nations studied--Mexico, Cuba, and Chile--a
fundamental shift in ideology and internal power coalitions shaped new
policies towards foreign-controlled enterprises that resulted in uncompensated expropriation of U. S. investments on a massive scale.
On the eve of expropriation, the economic problems of Mexico, Cuba,
and Chile were similar in that they experienced high degrees of
external dependency through international trade and the presence of
foreign direct investments in sensitive and strategic industries. They
attempted to eliminate the investment-dependency relationship through
wholesale expropriation of foreign-owned properties.

This summary chapter sets forth commonalities and differences among the three expropriation experiences with respect to the
following: (1) ideological issues leading to expropriation, (2) the
value of assets affected, (3) the legality of expropriatory actions, and
(4) U. S. policy responses, including the use of economic sanctions.

IDEOLOGICAL ISSUES

The massive penetration of the Mexican economy by U. S.,
British, and other foreign direct investments prior to the 1910
revolution generated a powerful nationalist reaction that ever since
has motivated Mexico's continuing quest for "economic independence."
The expropriation of U. S. investments in agriculture (1936), railways (1937), and petroleum (1938) was the most dramatic expression
of a persistent Mexican policy goal: "the reconquest of Mexico for
Mexicans." Since the presidential term of Lazaro Cardenas (1934-
40), Mexican policy towards multinational corporations has involved

striking a delicate balance between the country's objective need for foreign investment (and the associated managerial-technological resources) and the containment of such corporations within the bounds of an acceptable role in the economic life of the nation.

Cuba and Chile, before the political ascendance of their Marxist governments, succeeded in winning majority ownership and control over the premier export industry formerly dominated by U. S. investors. "Cubanization" of the sugar industry and "Chileanization" of the large copper mines were an accomplishment before the subsequent seizures and uncompensated expropriations of the Castro and Allende governments. "Cubanization" in the 1950s and "Chileanization" in the 1960s were pragmatic responses to nationalist aspirations in the two countries. Most important, these policy responses were compatible with the rule of law and sustained economic development. In Mexico, with the exception of the railways (which had been "Mexicanized" as early as 1902-09, during the latter phase of the Porfirian era), the petroleum and mining industries were over 95 percent foreign-dominated on the eve of President Cardenas' expropriatory actions.

In contrast with Mexico, the Marxist regimes of Fidel Castro and of the late President Salvador Allende envisioned the uncompensated expropriation of U. S.-controlled enterprises as merely a first step in the radical transformation of their societies.

Compared with other nations in Latin America, Cuba in the latter 1950s and Chile in the latter 1960s ranked high in the general level of living afforded their citizens. Before the advent of their Marxist governments, both nations experienced moderate rates of economic growth. In Mexico, the expropriation experience was preceded by nearly three decades of economic stagnation and political turmoil.

VALUE OF ASSETS AFFECTED

The estimated value of U. S.-owned investments expropriated in Mexico from 1936-38 exceeds $300 million, including $206 million in the oil industry. Between 1959 and 1960 the government of Cuba seized properties belonging to U. S. nationals with an estimated value of $1.8 billion (see Table 7.1). This magnitude is greater than the total amount expropriated by all other Communist countries combined, including the Soviet Union, Poland, Rumania, Czechoslovakia, Hungary, Yugoslavia, and Bulgaria. Of this sum, nearly $1.6 billion represents the certified claims of corporations; the value of properties taken from individuals is estimated at $221 million.

The estimated value of U. S. investments taken in Chile by the government of the late President Allende falls between $747

TABLE 7.1

Expropriation of U.S. Investments in Mexico, Cuba, and Chile: A Comparative View

	Cuba	Chile	Mexico
Capital losses	$1.8 billion	$747-833 million	$302 million
Domestic law	Circumvention of judicial system (unconstitutional)	Circumvention of judicial system; retroactive measures	Retroactive measures; ambiguity
International law	Departure from accepted standards	Departure from accepted standards	Departure from accepted standards
U.S. sanctions	Elimination of sugar quota and general trade embargo	Cessation of bilateral assistance; negative vote in multinational institutions; compensation link in context of debt renegotiations	None
Economic consequences (U.S.)	Reallocation of sugar quota. Capital losses shared by U.S. property owners and U.S. treasury	Capital losses shared by U.S. corporations, U.S. treasury, and possibly OPIC	Capital losses shared by U.S. oil companies and possibly U.S. treasury
Economic consequences (expropriating nation)	Major geographical trade diversion; spare parts crisis	No geographical trade diversion; international credit worthiness jeopardized	Temporary geographical trade diversion and reduction of oil exports
Settlement of claims	None	Return of many enterprises to original owners; agreements with OPIC and Cerro; discussions with Anaconda and Kennecott	Agreements reached on all claims between 1940-47

Source: Compiled by author.

million and $833 million. Of the total, the assets of the U. S. copper
mining companies range between $537 million and $623 million,
including notes repudiated by the Marxist government. The remaining
$210 million represents the equity investment of U. S. firms inter-
vened or requisitioned by Chile from 1971-73. Capital losses from
expropriation suffered by U. S. nationals in Cuba were estimated at
over twice the magnitude of U. S. investor losses in Chile (see Table
7.1). The substantial decline in the purchasing power of the U. S.
dollar from the latter 1930s to the early 1970s suggests that the real
value of expropriated properties in Mexico approximated $900 million
in terms of current dollars.

The U. S. government investment insurance program, managed
by the Overseas Private Investment Corporation (OPIC), was available to U. S. investors in both Cuba and Chile. A share of the $600
million investment expansion program (1967-71) for Chile's large
copper mines was insured against expropriation by the U. S. government. The investment insurance program did not become available
in Cuba until 29 November 1957, about a year before Castro's takeover of the island. The program was not authorized for existing
investments, and no contracts were issued on new commitments by
U. S. firms in Cuba. Capital losses stemming from expropriations in
both nations were shared by the affected U. S. property owners and
indirectly by the U. S. treasury. Additionally, because of the U. S.
government's exposure in Chile through the provision of expropriation
risk insurance, a part of the capital loss in that nation may also be
sustained by OPIC.

LEGALITY OF ACTIONS

The taking of U. S. -owned properties in Mexico, Cuba, and
Chile constituted a departure from accepted standards of international
law that require the payment of adequate, prompt, and effective compensation. In both Cuba and Chile, U. S. citizens and firms whose
properties were nationalized, intervened, or seized were denied the
right of recourse through the regular courts of law to the respective
supreme courts. In Chile, whenever lower courts ruled in favor of
firms intervened or seized by the state, the Marxist government
usually ignored these judicial decisions.

The seizures of U. S. corporate investments and properties
of individual U. S. citizens by the Castro regime did not conform to
domestic law. Article 24 of the Cuban constitution of 1940 guaranteed
protection of property on a nondiscriminatory basis and established
the juridical procedure for special cases involving expropriation.
Property could be expropriated only for just cause involving a public

utility or social interest, and then only through prior indemnification of the owner in cash as determined by the courts.

The presumed legal basis of the taking of U.S. properties in Cuba was contained in three decree laws: The Agrarian Reform Law of 3 June 1959, the Law of Nationalization of 6 July 1960, and Law 890 of 14 October 1960. A provision for compensation in 30-year bonds at two percent interest was contained in the Nationalization Law. However, compensation would not become effective unless the then prevailing American sugar quota of 3.2 million tons and the U.S. price of sugar were both raised. The practical effect of this provision was the effective nonpayment of all nationalized properties.

In Chile, the "integral nationalization" of the remaining U.S. investments in the large copper mines gives, on first reflection, the appearance of a concern for legal scruples. The measure was carried out through constitutional amendment approved by the Chilean Congress. However, as has been noted, the nationalization bill specifically denied the large U.S. copper mining companies the right of recourse through the regular courts of law to the Chilean Supreme Court. Further, the Special Copper Tribunal, created by authority of the amendment, denied the petitions of the U.S. companies for reconsideration of the deduction of alleged "excess profits" from any compensation paid them for their expropriated assets on grounds of "the absolute incompetence of the Court to know such matters."

Allende and his policymakers decided that the constitutional amendment was the only procedure whereby the state could release itself from the bindings placed on it by the "Chileanization" and "pacted nationalization" agreements. In brief, the Marxist regime had to "unmake" the work of President Eduardo Frei and insure that the "integral nationalization" of the large copper mines would not be "exposed to the interminable discussion before regular courts of justice."

The amendment authorized the president to make a series of deductions from the value of compensation including alleged "excess profits" earned by the U.S. companies from 1955-1970. Allende set the amount of "excess profits" that would be deducted from compensation to be paid to U.S. copper mining companies at $774 million or, according to his calculations, profits allegedly received over 12 percent of book value from 5 May 1955 (the date of the "New Deal" Law) and 31 December 1970. This deduction transformed the U.S. copper mining companies from creditors to debtors. Their assets and future earnings prospects were wiped out in a single political act.

First, it must be noted that the U.S. copper mining enterprises earned their profits in compliance with Chilean law and the terms of specific tax agreements concluded in 1955 and 1967. Their operations were monitored closely by the Chilean government. The deductions made for "excess profits" penalized the companies for acts that previous Chilean administrations officially approved. Since it is nowhere stated that the alleged "excess profits" are based on a violation of Chilean law, President Allende's administration effectively abrogated 16 years of tax legislation.

It was the position of the Allende government that the legal basis for the deduction of "excess profits" was not the acts themselves, but the allegation that there was an "unjust enrichment" for the U.S. copper mining companies deriving from those acts. The purpose of the deduction, therefore, was to introduce a "historical rectification" for an alleged wrong done against the Chilean economy over a period of years.

This leads to the second point, namely the accuracy of President Allende's calculations. My own conclusion, based on the analysis of profit and investment data, is that the average rate of return (net profits as a percent of U.S. equity) for the 1955-70 period was 12.4 percent--hardly an excessive rate for the mineral extraction sector and roughly equal to the "reasonable profit" cited by Allende. From this, the "excess profits" allegation seems to be without empirical foundation.

In Mexico legal controversy centered on article 27 of the constitution of 1917, which stipulates that subsoil mineral resources are the inalienable patrimony of the nation. The new constitution, reflecting strong nationalist feelings, raised an important question regarding the status of oil rights acquired by foreigners prior to 1917 under the mining laws of 1884, 1892, and 1909. In two instances, in 1921 and 1927, the Mexican Supreme Court ruled that the 1917 constitution was not retroactive with respect to the oil rights in the subsoil acquired by the companies prior to its adoption, provided that "positive acts" had been performed in exercising such rights. When the Mexican Congress, at the initiative of President Plutarco Calles, enacted in 1925 a petroleum law that required the foreign oil companies to exchange their subsoil titles of unlimited duration for 50-year concessions, the U.S. government exerted diplomatic pressure to have the retroactive provision of the law rescinded.

The legal basis for the oil expropriation decree of March 1938 was not article 27, but was instead the Expropriation Law of 1936 in the context of a critical labor dispute. When the Mexican Supreme Court subsequently affirmed the expropriatory action, it held that compensation due to the former owners could not include the capitalized value of the oil resources in the ground. Thus, the Supreme Court of Mexico reversed itself on the position taken in 1921 and 1927 regarding the retroactive application of article 27 in the 1917 constitution.

ECONOMIC SANCTIONS

In its posture toward Mexico, Cuba, and Chile, the U. S. government recognized the sovereign right of these nations to expropriate foreign-owned properties--provided that prompt, adequate, and effective compensation be given. In each instance, the United States declared its willingness to negotiate all disputes arising from the taking of American properties.

When negotiations proved to be ineffective, the United States applied economic sanctions against Cuba and Chile. In response to the Cuban seizures of American-owned properties, the United States eliminated the island's sugar import quota and declared a general trade embargo. The Chilean takings of U. S.-owned properties provoked a milder U. S. official response: cessation of bilateral economic assistance and the withholding of support from loans under consideration by multinational financial institutions, for example, the World Bank and the Inter-American Development Bank. In conformity with President Nixon's policy statement, "Economic Assistance and Investment Security in Developing Nations," the U. S. government linked Chile's request for renegotiation of its external debt to compensation for American properties taken.

The Franklin D. Roosevelt administration used its good office to bring the Mexican government and the U. S. oil companies to the conference table and to reach an amicable settlement. Beyond this point, the U. S. government refrained from deeper involvement in the Mexican oil controversy. Indeed, President Roosevelt may have weakened the bargaining position of the Sinclair Oil Co., Standard Oil Co. (N.J.), and the other American companies by conceding the Mexican contention that the underground oil should not be counted in the final compensation settlement.[1] J. Lloyd Mecham aptly summarizes the official U. S. position at that time.

> By not convenient resort to sophistry is it possible
> to obscure the fact that the president with the frank
> acquiescence of the New Deal, was allowed to scrap
> the Bucareli Agreement of 1923 and confiscate
> without compensation the underground oil resources
> belonging to the oil companies by legal acquisition.
> The plan for compensation worked out later in 1942
> was clearly based on the denial of any property
> rights in the petroleum underground. Those rights
> have been placed on the sacrificial altar of the Good
> Neighbor policy.[2]

Since 1960 the Soviet bloc, especially the USSR, has replaced the United States as Cuba's major customer and supplier. This fundamental geographical reorientation of the island's historical trade pattern led to a severe crisis in Cuba's ability to procure replacement parts for its U. S. -oriented capital stock. Chile, on the other hand, did not experience disruption of her trade pattern under the Allende government, for U. S. economic sanctions did not extend Chile's traditional trade relationships. However, Chile's international credit worthiness was adversely affected by the investment disputes.

The boycott of Mexican petroleum instigated in 1937 by the American and British oil companies forced Mexico temporarily to greatly reduce her oil shipments and to find alternative export markets in Germany and Italy.

NOTES

1. J. Lloyd Mecham, A Survey of United States-Latin American Relations (Boston: Houghton Mifflin, 1965), p. 369.
2. Ibid., p. 370.

8

U.S. INVESTMENTS AND INTER-AMERICAN RELATIONS: TOWARD A POLICY OF PRUDENTIAL DISENGAGEMENT

A key part of this "benign neglect" has been the development of the phrase "low profile." I have looked into the origins of the phrase; I am not completely sure from whence it comes, but I think it is a phrase used by designers of armoured vehicles to indicate the effort made to make a smaller target.
—David Bronheim, "Relations Between the United States and Latin America," International Affairs 46, no. 3 (July 1970): 510.

Uncompensated expropriation of properties belonging to U.S. nationals in Latin American has emerged as a vexing problem for U.S. policy. Beginning with the Cuban revolution there have occurred major expropriatory actions involving U.S. investment in Brazil (1959 and 1962), Argentina (1963), Peru (1968-74), Bolivia (1969), and Chile (1971-73). Although expropriations in Peru, Brazil, Argentina, and Bolivia were aimed predominantly at public utility and mineral holdings, in Cuba and Chile (under Marxist political leadership) takings of U.S. property affected the entire spectrum of economic activities: manufacturing, commerce, agriculture, and banking, as well as petroleum, utilities, and mining. As noted in Chapter 1, a conservative estimate of the value of U.S.-owned assets taken in Latin America during the 1959-74 period totals about $3.6 billion. Notwithstanding the successful delayed settlement of some of these cases, U.S. claims against Latin American governments as of April 1974 reached an impressive figure of $2.7 billion.

The United States has a responsibility to protect the property of its citizens abroad. Expropriatory actions of the nature cited above impair good international relations and cause strained relations to deteriorate further. Capital losses of this magnitude and the impairment of future earnings prospects dramatize the opportunity lost by Americans for secure investments at home.

This chapter evaluates U. S. investment policy toward Latin America in the perspective of the Alliance for Progress and the Nixon administration's "low profile" posture. It seeks to answer the question: how can the United States avoid or minimize investment disputes in a region where economic nationalism and Marxist ideological hostility influence the climate and the "rules of the game" for foreign investment? An evaluation of U. S. investment policy in relation to the nations of Latin America must consider both economic and geopolitical factors. The political factor has emphasized the role of private investment, including its associated managerial and technical capabilities, as a complement of U. S. governmental assistance to low income areas.

U. S. POLICIES

Among the major declared U. S. aims in Latin America in the period since World War II have been (1) the security of the hemisphere from external threats and the prevention of Marxist-Leninist regimes in the Americas; (2) encouragement of democratic institutions and economic and social progress in the Latin American nations; (3) the protection of the rights of U. S. citizens abroad including their legitimate property rights; (4) the maintenance of freedom of navigation, particularly through the Panama Canal; and (5) the maintenance of a cordial atmosphere that would foster U. S. influence and permit normal, mutually beneficial relations to flourish. [1] The United States has encouraged and protected American direct investment abroad partly for its instrumental role in advancing the area's economic and social development, including strengthening the region's private sector. Given the propensity of some Latin American nations to expropriate U. S. business holdings with little or no compensation, such official encouragement has dramatized the inconsistent and often irreconcilable nature of our diverse objectives in Latin America.

Benevolent Paternalism: The Alliance for Progress

The U. S. policymakers who supported the Alliance for Progress operated on the assumption that economic growth, social reform, and political democracy are mutually reinforcing aspects of an effective program of development. Andreas F. Lowenfeld, who served in

139

the legal adviser's office of the U. S. State Department in the early 1960s writes, "But the New Frontier, from the President down, believed that misery bred revolution, whereas economic growth, political democracy, and social justice would reinforce one another in the march toward attainment of our common ideals."[2] Accelerated economic and social development in Latin America, it was anticipated, would foster more stable political regimes friendly to the United States. An implicit assumption widely shared by the supporters of the alliance was that a higher per capita income, literacy, improved health, and other social gains would immunize Latin American societies against adopting a Marxist model of development. The security aspects of the alliance, writes Karl Schmitt, "were conceived in terms of 'buying time' in the several Latin American countries until greater economic and social benefits could become available to the masses thereby undercutting Soviet, Castroite, and other revolutionary anti-U. S. appeals."[3]

By encouraging U. S.-based multinational corporations to invest in the region's development, the policymakers must also have assumed that those changes would not effect the security of properties owned by American citizens. Under both the Kennedy and Johnson administrations, political risk insurance against expropriation was offered on liberal terms through the Agency for International Development (AID) to U. S. investors in Latin America.

It should be remembered that President-elect Kennedy's Task Force on Latin America, which recommended (among other things) the creation of the Alliance for Progress, was much more modest than the alliance charter in its forecast of what could be accomplished through the alliance in 10 years.[4] Moreover, the task force's report recommended the formation of a broad political front that would bring together "the various Latin American political parties covering a spectrum as wide as Catholic and moderate democratic parties on the right, running to Christian Socialist and non-Communist Socialist parties on the left. . . ."[5] The alliance was a highly publicized, well-intentioned, cooperative undertaking of the United States in its relations with Latin America. Although several of its specified targets were reached, it also raised unwarranted hopes followed by frustration.

Beyond New Frontier Activism: The "Low Profile"

It has been widely acknowledged that the activist Kennedy formula of large scale U. S. assistance and diplomatic support for the Latin American "democratic left" was replaced by President Nixon's policy of the "low profile." U. S. policy under Nixon rested on the premise that the ability of this nation is limited sharply in achieving its long-term goals in Latin America. The social and cultural forces blocking broad economic development and constitutional democracy in many Latin American countries are far older than the "Colossus of the North;"[6] hence, it would be imprudent for the United States to promise what it cannot deliver.

Taking into account these fundamental realities together with the intensification of economic nationalism and expropriation in several Latin American countries, the Republican administration deliberately reduced the visibility of the U. S. on the hemispheric stage.[7] Increasingly, aid was channeled through multinational institutions. In the mid-1960s, roughly two-thirds of our aid to Latin America was bilateral; under Nixon, the proportion was reversed and two-thirds of our aid flowed through multinational organizations such as the Inter-American Development Bank, the World Bank, and the United Nations Development Program.[8] The United States also untied its bilateral development loans to free them for procurement in other countries. In 1972, the United States took a leading role in lifting a requirement of the Inter-American Development Bank that all new members must belong to the Organization of American States. This step opened the way for Canada's entry into the bank in May of that year. A specific recommendation to multilateralize the economic relations of Latin American with the world was included in the Peterson Report issued at the end of 1971.[9] The report argues that it is in our own interest, as well as that of Latin America, to bring more aid and investment from other industrialized countries and open markets in other countries for products of Latin America.

In his address before the Inter-American Press Association, President Nixon said, "We will not encourage U. S. private investment where it is not wanted, nor where local political conditions face it with unwarranted risks."[10] When intractable investment disputes arise, the Nixon administration favored a range of impartial settlement procedures, especially international adjudication or arbitration.[11] Consequently, support for the International Center for the Settlement of Investment Disputes (ICSID) was one of the touchstones of U. S. policy under Nixon's administration.

During the early months of 1974 the United States proposed a "new dialogue" with Latin America. As evidence that the United States was moving toward a new hemispheric policy, Secretary of State Henry Kissinger cited recent agreements with Mexico on water salinity, with Panama on the canal, and with Peru on expropriation of mines, factories, and agricultural estates. In an address delivered before the OAS General Assembly on April 20, 1974, Kissinger reaffirmed the "special relationship" with Latin America and pledged, "We will do our utmost to expand Latin American access to United

States markets, to maintain our assistance levels, and to consult on political and economic issues of common concern."[12] Noting that U. S. private investment in the hemisphere has at times been a source of friction, he indicated that the United States would join with the Latin American states in a study commission that would prepare guidelines applicable to the conduct of multinational enterprises.

POLICY INSTRUMENTS

OPIC: Stimulating Direct Investment
Through Political Risk Insurance

The investment insurance program has become a major instrument by which the United States has sought to stimulate direct investments in less developed countries. Originating as part of the Economic Cooperation Act of 1948, the program insured U. S. firms against war, the inconvertibility of currencies, and, beginning in 1950, the political risk of expropriation. In January 1971 Congress created the Overseas Private Investment Corporation (OPIC), an independent U. S. government corporation, to assume the political risk insurance functions previously handled by the Agency for International Development (AID).

During the formative years, OPIC was forced to concentrate an inordinate amount of attention on the solution of inherited problems. These arose primarily from the uncompensated expropriation of U. S.-owned properties in Chile, Bolivia, and Peru. At the time it opened its doors for business, OPIC had only $85 million in its insurance reserve and faced some $420 million in potential claims.[13] OPIC insurance covers only new investments or additions to existing productive facilities and must have approval of the host government. In the event the U. S. investor is not paid under the program, the U. S. government is recognized as the succeeding claimant; and direct negotiations for settlement will be undertaken between the two governments.

By providing loan guarantees and expropriation risk insurance, OPIC substantially enhances the U. S. firm's incentive to invest abroad. The availability of political risk insurance may be a critical element in the investor's decision to take his capital to a low income nation. A Business International survey of nearly 400 American companies revealed that 46 percent of the respondents indicated that political risk insurance was a necessary step in their decision to invest in a less developed country, and 70 percent of the respondents in the extractive field viewed such insurance as an essential precondition to going forward with a project.[14]

Expropriation, unlike fire or auto accidents, cannot be determined by the law of averages; there exists no actuarial basis or principle of large numbers for calculating the potential liability; a specified premium cannot be related to the risk of expropriation.* Consequently, the insurance reserve was not intended by Congress to cover catastrophic losses, such as when a country, heavily endowed with U.S. investments, expropriates these properties without adequate compensation and without regard for international law and practice. Expropriation insurance contracts are backed by the full faith and credit of the United States.

The investment insurance program shifts the risk of expropriation from the American firm to the United States government and potentially to the American taxpayer. On the eve of the Chilean expropriations, OPIC's total investment reserve fund of $85 million in 1970 was substantially lower than the amount of expropriation insurance written for Chile alone ($283 million).[15] To close the gap between claims and reserves, OPIC early in 1972 requested Congress to raise its reserves to $200 million. The Chilean committment did not include the additional $154 million claim of the Anaconda Company against OPIC related to the company's former Chilean investments (see Chapter 5). The ousting of the Allende government in September 1973 probably saved OPIC from an embarrassing financial predicament. Both Anaconda's $154 million claim and the claim for $92.5 million filed by ITT in connection with the expropriation of the Chile Telephone Company were denied by the OPIC Board of Directors.** Both of these companies disputed OPIC's denial and have submitted the cases to arbitration under the rules of the American Arbitration Association.

---

*Nevertheless, private insurance companies do write confiscation insurance to a very limited extent. For example, a new specialist company, Investment Insurance International (III), associated with Lloyds of London, obtains a large volume of political risk insurance business well spread by nationality of ownership, location, and type of industry. As a general rule, III writes only 12-month policies and gives coverage only if the assured can exercise control over the management of those assets. Information provided by R.A.G. Jackson, manager, Union-America Management Co., Ltd.

**In the case of ITT, OPIC denied the claim for "violations of the insurance contract." In the decision announced April 1973, OPIC cited ITT's failure to comply with its obligation to disclose material information as required by the terms of its OPIC contracts.

A recent General Accounting Office Study of OPIC concluded that the corporation practices sound risk management in the conduct of its insurance programs and that OPIC management had made "good progress" in project selectivity. [16] Compared with its predecessor agency, AID's Office of Private Resources, OPIC has taken a series of preventive measures to minimize political risks of U.S. investments abroad. These include, in addition to the reinsurance agreement with Lloyds of London, its limitation on the growth of further exposure in countries of heavy concentration and its requirement that investors assume a part of the risk in large or sensitive projects. The company's expropriation portfolio as of 1973 had a current exposure of $2.4 billion, of which $410 million was reinsured with Lloyd's, leaving a net exposure of $2 billion. Of the global expropriation insurance outstanding, 56 percent was in Latin America. [17]

By statute, OPIC's major objective is fostering economic and social development in the less developed countries. On the other hand, Congress increasingly is directing the corporation's management to work toward a self-sustaining organization that would place no demands on the American taxpayer. The report issued by the Senate Subcommittee on Multinational Corporations proposes transfer of the insurance program to U.S. private insurance companies on a schedule spelled out in draft legislation. [18] Its assumption that the insurance industry is willing and able to do this on the basis proposed in the subcommittee's detailed legislation has been denied by industry leaders. At variance with the report, many business leaders argue for a greatly expanded OPIC role in the Third World. For example, Ronald K. Shelp, executive secretary of the Association of American Chambers of Commerce in Latin America (AACCLA), in testimony before the House Subcommittee on Foreign Economic Policy urged Congress to encourage OPIC to use less selectivity in its risk management, allowing a greater flow of U.S. private capital into low income countries and higher risk ventures. [19] OPIC's management is thus caught up in a dilemma arising out of its ambiguous charges.

The Foreign Tax Credit

Economic analysis suggests that the private comparison of the rate of return (profit) on investment abroad with that at home is inappropriate for guiding the allocation of savings in the national interest. [20] First, the risk of confiscation or repudiation of loans affect the individual firm whether its investments are at home or abroad. But the nation as a whole retains in the first case the investment and the earnings thereof, while in the second case both are lost. Second, there is a revenue loss to the U.S. government whenever a

U. S. -based corporation invests abroad rather than at home. All other things being equal, an investment in another country by an American-based multinational corporation benefits the national interest only if <u>after-tax</u> earnings abroad exceed net earnings <u>before taxes</u> in the United States.

In deciding where to invest, the private firm compares expected after-tax profit in the United States and abroad, since it is a matter of indifference to it which government receives the tax. Under U. S. tax law, earnings of a U. S. subsidiary abroad are granted a foreign tax credit equal to the tax paid in the source country. This provision, while eliminating double taxation, deprives the U. S. treasury of revenues it otherwise would have received. * Clearly, the tax law establishes a bias for investment abroad, because a U. S. corporate taxpayer operating in another country may <u>credit</u> foreign income taxes against his federal tax liaibility, while a domestic subsidiary may only <u>deduct</u> state and city income taxes. (For example, firms operating in Minnesota or Pennsylvania, where corporate tax rates exceed 10 percent, must deduct rather than credit those state income taxes.)

The average after-tax yield of U. S. direct investments in Latin America in 1960-69 of 13. 5 percent would at first glance appear to compare favorably with the 10.4 percent private rate of return of large U. S. corporations operating in this country. [21] However, assuming a corporation income tax rate of 50 percent applicable both at home and abroad, the rate of return to the U. S. economy would be 20. 8 percent (profits before federal income taxes) on investments located <u>within</u> the nation compared with only 13. 5 percent for U. S. direct investments located in the Latin American area.

EVALUATION OF U. S. POLICIES

Accelerated economic and social development in Latin America, to which U. S. official assistance and direct investments have contributed, did not necessarily foster in the area more stable constitutional regimes friendly to the United States. Further, particularly in Chile and Peru, the Alliance for Progress proposals for agrarian and tax reform led to the withdrawal of local conservative support for U. S. -owned enterprises. Large landowners and businessmen in these

---

*When it comes to the timing of tax liability, U. S. tax law makes a distinction between "branches" and "subsidiaries. " For further discussion of the foreign tax credit and the so-called tax "deferral, " see Virgil Salera, <u>Multinational Business</u> (Boston: Houghton Mifflin Co. , 1969), pp. 143-48.

countries reasoned that if they could be deprived of their properties
without what they considered to be adequate compensation, so could
U.S. firms. In promoting the flow of U.S. investments to Latin
America in the 1960s, the United States may have magnified the number and intensity of bilateral investment disputes, both current and
prospective.

The evidence offered in support of a positive relationship
between economic and social development on the one hand and political stability and constitutional order on the other is at best ambiguous. [22] Samuel P. Huntington, for example, argues that in poor
nations a positive relationship exists between the rate of economic
growth and political instability and, further, that social mobilization
is even more destabilizing than economic development. In Huntington's words, "Modernization breeds instability."[23]

It is interesting to note that the poorest nations—Haiti, Bolivia, and Paraguay—have not become Marxist-oriented; and Cuba and
Chile (until the military coup of September 1973), among the socially
and economically most advanced nations in Latin America, followed
this path. Chile received the highest amount of U.S. economic assistance per capita during the Alliance for Progress decade 1961-70; and
Cuba, until mid-1960, was the recipient of a substantial U.S. subsidy
in the form of the premium price offered for the island's sugar.* We
have also shown that both Cuba and Chile received large flows of U.S.
direct investments during the five or six years preceding the establishment of their Marxist regimes. This is not to argue that economic
assistance and foreign direct investments were linked causally to the
emergence of Marxist governments. The course of events in Cuba and
Chile, however, casts doubt on what has been one of the basic assumptions of our foreign assistance and investment promotion programs,
namely, that economic and social development is an effective antidote
against Marxism-Leninism in the low income nations. [24]

An evaluation of U.S. investment policies toward Latin America touches on three key elements as they affect the American economy:
(1) a comparison of the rates of return and of the risk of expropriation both at home and abroad, (2) the security of supply and relative
cost of petroleum resources at home and abroad, and (3) the impact
on American exports of U.S. investments in manufacturing affiliates
abroad.

The national rate of return of large corporations operating in
the United States, as we have noted, exceeds by a significant margin

---

*Altogether the sugar premium and the preferential tariff were
worth about $150 million a year to Cuba. See Leland L. Johnson, "U.S.
Business Interest in Cuba and the Rise of Castro," World Politics 28,
no. 2, (April 1965): 454.

the after-tax rate of return on U. S. investments in Latin America. And this differential in favor of domestic investment does not include an accounting of the massive capital losses of U. S.-based multinational companies arising out of expropriation in Latin America. On the other hand, American investments abroad benefit the home economy insofar as they stimulate U. S. exports. Recent data indicate that over half of all exports of manufactured products from the United States flow from American-based multinational corporations and about half of these go from the parent to the subsidiary plant abroad. [25] This suggests that the operation of U. S. firms abroad (including Latin America) stimulate increased exports from the United States that would have been impossible without the foreign plants. The choice, therefore, is often not between U. S. and foreign operations, but between foreign operations and no operations at all. *

U. S. direct investments in Latin American mineral development have been officially encouraged both to strengthen the economies of the host nations and to secure for the United States growing supplies of oil, copper, iron ore, and so forth at low marginal cost. About 34 percent of U. S. business holdings in Latin America at the end of 1972 were concentrated in extractive industries—24 percent in petroleum and 10 percent in mining and smelting. [26] However, the new international realities of the 1970s indicate that greater self-sufficiency in meeting the energy requirements of the U. S. is a course more appropriate to the national interest. The arguments in favor of a low U. S. foreign dependency posture in regard to its future energy needs are persuasive. [27] A determined effort by the United States to reduce its dependence on foreign oil should be welcomed by Western Europe and Japan, for they are faced with shrinking domestic sources and rapidly growing demands for oil. It would eliminate the capacity of major oil exporting nations at some future time to extract political concessions from the United States in its conduct of foreign policy. Access to politically secure reserves of mineral fuels has become a major problem as dramatized by the Arab oil embargo following the 1973 Middle Eastern conflict. And finally, the Organization of Petroleum Exporting Countries (OPEC), which includes Venezuela and Ecuador, may continue to cancel out the beneficial advantages of low cost oil production in the source countries through coordinated monopoly action to raise prices. Considering the huge and growing domestic

---

*American companies finding their exports blocked by national tariffs or quotas have responded defensively by investing in production facilities within the Latin American nations. A defensive investment to surmount tariff walls is often reinforced by the necessity to prevent market preemption by a competitor. U. S. investments in manufacturing

claims on U.S. capital resources* for improving the physical environment and developing indigenous energy sources, the United States can ill afford to encourage the outflow of investment to nations offering questionable security of property. On balance, then, there exist no compelling political or economic reasons for officially promoting U.S. direct investments in Latin America.

An investment dispute between a U.S. subsidiary and Latin American state could lead to one of several resolutions or actions. The American firm could (1) seek remedy in the local courts, (2) agree to negotiate differences, or (3) seek redress through international conciliation and arbitration. However, the absence of an independent judiciary in most Latin American republics indicates that the courts cannot be expected to provide an objectively fair settlement on litigation involving a U.S. affiliate and a Latin American government. And in Chile (where the judiciary has traditionally enjoyed considerable autonomy), a constitutional amendment (see Chapters 5 and 6) specifically denied the large U.S.-owned copper companies the right of recourse through the regular courts of law to the Chilean Supreme Court. Further, not a single Latin American nation (see Chapter 1) has been willing to resort to international arbitration and conciliation through the International Center for the Settlement of Investment Disputes or to participate in the International Insurance Agency proposed by the World Bank.

Should all of these remedies—local adjudication, negotiation, or international arbitration—fail to yield a reasonable settlement, then economic retaliation by the U.S. government likely would be the next step. President Nixon's statement on investment security (see Chapter 6) gives definition and visibility to U.S. policy on uncompensated expropriation. In clearly indicating that the United States is prepared to invoke economic sanctions for unacceptable behavior, other nations contemplating seizure of U.S.-owned property may restrain from carrying out such action. On the other hand, once an expropriatory action has taken place in a country such as Peru or Chile, economic sanctions by the United States actually may strengthen the hand of xenophobic nationalists, thereby triggering an unintended negative response.

---

affiliates in Latin America have been concentrated in those countries with large, protected, and growing markets.

*The First National Bank of Chicago estimates that the petroleum industry must spend $250 billion in the U.S. to add the new capital facilities needed between 1974 and 1985. Exxon News (13 May 1974).

CONCLUSIONS

In the long view, U. S. policy should aim at <u>preventing</u> the emergence of investment disputes and capital losses through uncompensated expropriation. Economic nationalism, Marxist ideological hostility, and the search for scapegoats influence the investment climate in a number of Spanish American nations. Whenever U. S. investors encounter some of these factors in combination, their position becomes exceedingly vulnerable. In this kind of situation, the prudent course for U. S. policy is not to encourage U. S. direct investments in the area.* Confrontations over the treatment of U. S. firms in some nations south of the Rio Grande exacerbate the already difficult and sensitive U. S.-Latin American relations. The "tension generated by the presence of U. S.-controlled subsidiaries abroad," as Raymond Vernon makes clear, "can hardly be thought of as an equivocal and positive contribution to U. S. foreign relations."[28] Such conflicts are not in the interest of the concerned parties: the U. S. government, the Latin American countries, and investors themselves.

The United States should avoid being maneuvered into the role of scapegoat for problems and discontents over which it has no control. For several decades, the dominant position of U. S. corporations among foreign investment sources in such nations as Mexico, Cuba, Argentina, Chile, and Venezuela has served as a convenient lightning rod for local politicians wishing to channel social frustrations into "safe" channels. The Special Latin American Coordinating Commission (CECLA), to illustrate this point, exonerates its member nations of any responsibility for underdevelopment, throwing the blame on the United States.[29]

With the rapid growth of Japanese, West German, and other foreign business investment in the area—and the decline of the American share—it will be more difficult to cast the United States as the

---

*At the same time, U. S. businessmen would be stimulated to find more flexible forms of association to reduce the possibility of later disputes. Examples of such forms include licensing and leasing arrangements, management contracts, and multinational private investment banks, for example, the Atlantic Community Development Group for Latin America (ADELA) and the newly organized Latin American Agri-business Development Corporation (LAAD). These approaches, by contrast with direct investment, provide Latin American private enterprise with advanced managerial and technical knowledge at minimum political risk to the U. S. enterprise.

unique culprit for the problems of some Latin American countries. *
Significantly, Brazil is the only Latin American nation in which the
U.S. share represents less than one-half of total foreign direct investments outstanding. The devaluations of the U.S. dollar in the
early 1970s should accelerate the trend toward a diminishing U.S.
share and a growing European and Japanese share of foreign investment in the region.

The Overseas Private Investment Corporation (OPIC) should
limit its coverage of additional political risk insurance to nations that
have chosen membership in the International Center for the Settlement
of Investment Disputes. The foreign tax credit and expropriation risk
insurance, in combination, promote an unwarranted flow of U.S.
investment to politically sensitive nations. The more restricted use
of official expropriation insurance would induce U.S. firms to make
a more careful evaluation of the political risk in prospective invest-
ment-receiving nations.

The United States looks with favor on the formulation of investment codes that provide "principles of behavior" to be observed by
multinational companies. The United Nations, the Organization for
Economic Cooperation and Development, and the Organization of
American States currently are drafting such codes. However, in the
light of the recent pattern of expropriations of foreign-owned properties in less developed countries, the United States should insist strongly
that such investment codes also should incorporate principles of
acceptable behavior to be observed by "host" nations.

In conclusion, an official investment policy of prudential dis-
engagement would mitigate the vexing problem of protecting the legitimate property rights of U.S. citizens in Latin America and offset
the rhetorical initiatives of the Marxist left in the region. It would
encourage the investment of new U.S. venture capital into sectors of
highest priority at home, rather than abroad. Finally, by coming to
terms with the current expression of economic nationalism in the
area, such a policy would improve the prospects for maintaining cordial and mutually beneficial relations with the nations of Latin America.

---

*By mid-1971 over half of Japan's $4 billion overseas invest-
ment was in the less developed nations. Japan projects foreign investments of $11 billion by 1975, and an astounding $26 billion by
1980. Its investments in less developed countries are growing already
at an annual rate of 25 percent, against only 5-6 percent for the
United States. Overseas Private Investment Corporation Topics 2,
no. 3 (June 1972): 8.

NOTES

1. The sources for identification of these aims include speeches of key administration officials published in the State Department Bulletins and Congressional Hearings. See Frank R. Pancake, "An Analysis of the U.S. Military Assistance Mission in Latin America," a paper delivered at the Southeastern Conference on Latin American Studies, 4 April 1970, Columbia, S.C., p. 4. See also Sidney Weintraub, "U.S. Policy Toward a Changing Latin America," Department of State Bulletin 64, no. 4 (26 April 1971): 550-54.

2. Andreas F. Lowenfeld, "Reflections on Expropriation and the Future of Investment in the Americas," The International Lawyer 7, no. 1 (January 1973): 117.

3. Karl M. Schmitt, "U.S. Security Interests in Latin America," a background paper for the Conference on Latin American-United States Economic Relations, 18-21 March 1973, Austin, Texas, p. 12.

4. Arthur P. Whitaker, "The Wailing Wall, or Pan American Tragedy in Two Acts," Orbis 15, no. 2 (Summer 1971): 696.

5. Ibid., p. 697.

6. See David C. Anderson's review article, "Latin Policy: Time for Benign Neglect?," Wall Street Journal, 23 October 1970, p. 17.

7. "U.S. Foreign Policy for the 1970s: Shaping of a Durable Peace, a report to the Congress by Richard Nixon, president of the United States, Washington, D.C., 3 May 1973, p. 116.

8. Ibid., p. 124.

9. Peter G. Peterson, The United States in the Changing World Economy, A Foreign Economic Perspective, Vol. I (Washington, D.C.: Government Printing Office, 27 December 1971), p. 28.

10. Action for Progress for the Americas, an address by Richard M. Nixon, Dept. of State Publication 8501 (Washington, D.C.: Government Printing Office, 1969, p. 8.

11. See William P. Rogers, "U.S. Policy Toward Latin America," a speech delivered on 12 April 1972 before the General Assembly of the Organization of American States, Washington, D.C.

12. Good Partner Policy for Americas, address by Secretary of State Henry A. Kissinger before the General Assembly of the Organization of American States, 20 April 1974, Atlanta, Georgia, p. 3.

13. Overseas Private Investment Corporation Annual Report Fiscal 1973, Washington, D.C.

14. Cited in Ronald K. Shelp, executive secretary of the Association of American Chambers of Commerce in Latin America

(AACCLA), Statement before the sub-committee on Foreign Economic Policy of the Committee on Foreign Affairs, U.S. House of Representatives, 13 June 1973, Washington, D.C., p. 5.

15. Investing in Developing Countries (Paris: Organization for Economic Cooperation and Development, 1970), p. 101, table 2.

16. OPIC Topics 2, no. 3 (September 1973): 6.

17. OPIC Annual Report, op. cit.

18. Ibid.

19. Shelp, op. cit.

20. See J. Carter Murphy, "International Investment and the National Interest," The Southern Economic Journal 27, no. 1 (July 1960); and Mordechai E. Kreinin, International Economics: A Policy Approach (New York: Harcourt, Brace, Jovanovich, 1971), pp. 330-42.

21. Earnings after taxes paid in Latin America are derived from Herbert K. May and Jose Antonio Fernandez Arena, Impact of Foreign Investment in Mexico (New York and Washington: National Chamber Foundation and Council of the Americas, 1972), p. 81, table 30. U.S. earnings after federal income taxes for 1964-71 are derived from Monthly Economic Letter, First National City Bank of New York, April issues, 1966-72 (period covered is 1964-71).

22. On this question see Martin C. Needler, Political Development in Latin America: Instability, Violence and Evolutionary Change (New York: Random House, 1968), ch. 4; and Samuel P. Huntington, Political Order in Changing Societies (New Haven and London: Yale University Press, 1968), pp. 49-59.

23. Huntington, op. cit., p. 57.

24. On this point, see George Wythe, The United States and Inter-American Relations (Gainesville: University of Florida Press, 1964), p. 219.

25. The United States in the Changing World Economy, Background Material, Vol. II (Washington, D.C.: Government Printing Office, 21 December 1971), p. 47.

26. Survey of Current Business (September 1973): 26-27, table 8A.

27. See Carroll L. Wilson, "A Plan for Energy Independence," Foreign Affairs 51, no. 4 (July 1973).

28. Raymond Vernon, "The Multinational Enterprise: Power Versus Sovereignty," Foreign Affairs 49, no. 4 (July 1971): 742.

29. Andres Suarez, "CECLA and the Latin American Regional Subsystem," a paper delivered at the 15th Annual Conference of the Rocky Mountain Social Science Association, 26-28 April 1973, Laramie, Wyoming, p. 16.

9

IMPLICATIONS OF THE
CHILEAN MILITARY COUP:
A POSTSCRIPT

The overthrow of President Allende's Marxist government on 11 September 1973 marked an important change in the relations between Chile and foreign investors. Among the high priorities of the new military regime headed by General Augusto Pinochet Ugarte was a reversal in Chile's economic deterioration and restoration of the nation's credit worthiness abroad. The new Chilean government had undertaken four measures aimed at restoration of business confidence. First, it agreed to pay its obligations to the Overseas Private Investment Corporation (OPIC) in connection with promissory notes originally held by Kennecott Copper Corporation and other American firms with affiliates in Chile. Second, it has returned factories and other enterprises that had been taken over without payment by the Marxist regime. Third, it decreed a Code of Foreign Investments to attract new venture capital from abroad. Finally, the military junta entered into serious conversations with Anaconda, Kennecott, and Cerro regarding compensation for the nationalized copper mining properties.

By August 1974 all major expropriated American-owned firms had been returned to their original owners except the $6 million Ford Motor Company assembly plant.[1] Ford is waiting for Chile to formulate a national automotive policy. Before resuming management control, the former owners had to sign a contract with the Government Development Corporation (CORFO) in which the owner pledged[2]

- to accept all liabilities, including debts incurred by the company while under state control;
- to make no claim for damage done to plant or installations, or any other form of claim, against the government administrators and to assume the cost of any repairs needed to get the plant back into full production.

- to honor all agreements reached with workers on wages and conditions; and
- to abide by the regulations contained in the "social statute" on which the government is now working.

Some of the most important names in U. S. industry stand to benefit from the decision to return the illegally seized companies to their owners. Among the firms included are Corning Glass Works, General Electric Company, and Dow Chemical. The latter owns several chemical and petrochemical plants in Chile valued at over $30 million. * The problems facing management in resuming operations of these enterprises are considerable. In most instances routine maintenance was overlooked, foreign exchange to purchase spare parts abroad was unavailable, and worker discipline was affected seriously by the lax management of the state bureaucracy.

The new military regime did not return the large copper mines to their pre-Allende joint venture status. However, the Chilean government appointed Julio Phillippi, a university law professor and former finance minister, to deal with Anaconda and Kennecott on the legal and constitutional aspects of the "integral nationalization."

After almost three years of negotiations with two Chilean governments, Cerro Corporation reached an agreement with the Pinochet regime providing compensation for its Andina mine. Under the agreement concluded in March 1974, Cerro will be paid $3. 2 million in cash, and $38. 6 million in 17-year notes, plus interest. OPIC has agreed to guarantee a portion of these notes, which will be fully guaranteed by the Central Bank of Chile. [3] Significantly, Cerro will continue to provide technical and engineering services to the mine's management as it has done since Andina was expropriated in 1971. The compensation covers Cerro's 70 percent equity ownership in Compania Mineral Andina, S. A. C. Gordon Murphy, president of Cerro, said that he "considered the settlement a reasonable one under the circumstances, and that the negotiations which had often been hard-fought and complex were cordial and fair. "[4]

The Chilean government announced on 27 July 1974 that an agreement with Anaconda was reached with respect to the 1971 expropriation of the Chuquicamata and El Salvador mining properties in

---

* Dow estimates that it will take several months to bring all plants back to full production. In addition to paying $1. 5 million worth of physical repairs, the Chilean companies will have to honor some $500, 000 in unpaid bills and other expenses run up by the former government managers. Herbert E. Meyer, "Dow Picks Up the Pieces in Chile, " Fortune (April 1974), p. 148.

Chile.[5] Under the settlement, Anaconda's subsidiaries, Chile Exploration Company and Andes Copper Mining Company, received a cash payment of about $65 million and $188 million in 10-year promissory notes of Corporacion del Cobre guaranteed by the Central Bank of Chile.[6] These notes bear interest at 10 percent per annum, subject to Chilean income tax at the rate of 40 percent. The $253 million settlement leaves Anaconda free to continue the arbitration of its claims against OPIC with respect to the 1971 expropriation. As a result of the accord, all prior claims and controversies between the company and the Chilean government have been resolved. This includes disposal of all claims for Chilean taxes and other matters, all legal actions in Chile and the United States and all claims with respect to the notes previously issued to Anaconda's subsidiaries at the end of 1969.

Considering Chile's extremely difficult international financial position, the Cerro and Anaconda settlements appear to be fair and generous. A Kennecott Copper Corporation spokesman said that his company, also, is in the process of negotiation for a settlement.[7]

The Anaconda settlement followed the announcement of a new Code of Foreign Investments that guarantees nondiscriminatory treatment of foreign investments, particularly in determination of taxable income, customs duties, quotas and allocations, and foreign exchange treatment for exports and imports.[8] While improving the domestic climate for investment, the Chilean government would like to amend the foreign investment code of the Andean Pact of which Chile is a member nation. Thus, Raul Saenz, Minister of Economy and Coordination, has been touring Andean capitals to induce the Andean Pact members to moderate the pact's "Decision 24" which sets tough restrictions on ownership participation and profit remittances of multinational corporations.

After only a year in power, the Pinochet government could point to some tangible results: Production in the large copper mines was moving ahead rapidly, Chilean technicians were returning to their country, large new foreign investment projects were under consideration, and Chile's international credit worthiness was improving significantly.

NOTES

1. "Chile: A Wobbly Economy Needs Foreign Help," Business Week, August 3, 1974, pp. 30-31.
2. Latin American Economic Report 2, no. 4 (25 January 1974): 15.
3. OPIC Topics 3, no. 2 (April 1974): 3.

4. Ibid.

5. Diario Official de la Republica de Chile, Santiago, 24 July 1974, p. 1.

6. "Anaconda Settles with Chilean Government," News from the Anaconda Company, New York, 24 July 1974.

7. "Anaconda Says Chile to Pay it $253 Million Sum," Wall Street Journal, 25 July, 1974, p. 7.

8. Embassy of Chile, Summary of Recent Events, no. 265 (July-August 1974).

ARGENTINA

In 1958, the year Arturo Frondizi assumed the Argentine presidency, a public monopoly, Yacimento Petroliferos Fiscales (YPF), was supplying only one-third of the country's oil needs. Frondizi and his economic advisers, guided by a compelling need to get the economy off dead center, awarded contracts to several American petroleum firms and the Royal-Dutch Shell group. Argentina continued to claim ownership of the oil. From 1958-62 Argentine petroleum output tripled as the foreign-owned companies produced in their own contract areas or helped YPF in its drilling and exploration operations. By the end of 1962, Argentina had become nearly self-sufficient in petroleum production; the foreign companies were saving the country $300 million in foreign exchange annually.

According to a report of the board of directors of YPF to the National Congress, the cost of YPF-produced oil was more than double the price per barrel paid the foreign companies for oil delivered.[1] The cost of the YPF produced oil, for example, was reported to be $3.58 per barrel, compared with the contract price for oil delivered by Pan American International Oil Co. ($1.58 per barrel, which also included transportation over a greater distance).

The subsequent administration of President Arturo Illia moved on 15 November 1963 to annul the exploration and development contracts awarded to the foreign firms from 1958-61. It accused the Frondizi government of violating the Argentine Constitution and of making economically harmful deals in signing the contracts. Antulio Pozzio, then secretary of fuels and energy, told a congressional investigating committee that there "will neither be renegotiation of the contracts nor indemnification," but Facundo Suarez, head of YPF, who was regarded as an exponent of the moderate line, indicated that Argentina might pay from $70-100 million to reimburse the foreign companies for their investment or "at worst," in the event of a loss in the courts, $150 million.[2] The U.S. oil companies alone claimed an investment in Argentina of over $200 million. The sharp reversal in Argentina's petroleum policy portended eventual loss of the nation's recently achieved self-sufficiency in oil.

In 1967, a few months after the installation by military coup of General Ongonia as president, an amicable out-of-court settlement was negotiated between the foreign-producing companies and the government. Cash settlements to six U.S. firms (Cities Service, Esso,

Pan American, Tenneco, Transworld Drilling, and Union Oil),
usually in the form of notes discounted by foreign banks, ranged from
about $4 million for Transworld to about $42 million each for Esso
and Pan American.[3] Following the disposition of claims, some of the
foreign companies continued operating in Argentina under provisions
of a new, liberal oil law.

BOLIVIA

On 17 October 1969 the regime of General Alfredo Ovando
Candia, without warning, expropriated Gulf Oil Company's Bolivian
oil and gas fields and seized its facilities.[4] Since entering Bolivia
in 1955 under a 40-year concession, Gulf had invested $150 million
and dealt with six successive governments in compliance with the
nation's petroleum code. The company made its first oil discovery in
1960. During the entire period in which Gulf operated in Bolivia,
it had no operating profits; yet during the same period, the Bolivian
government received nearly $18 million from Gulf in royalties, taxes,
and other payments.[5]

Due to Bolivia's landlocked geographic position, export of
petroleum moved through a 600-mile pipeline system from Eastern
Bolivian fields across the Altiplano to the Chilean port of Arica on the
Pacific, where the oil then moved by tankers to refineries in California. At the moment of expropriation, Gulf's Bolivian subsidiary
and YPFB, the state oil company, were completing an agreement
whereby the two companies would explore jointly acreage located in
the Altiplano area of Bolivia. The two firms also had formed a joint
venture with World Bank support whose purpose was to own and operate
a 329-mile gas pipeline from Bolivia's Santa Cruz fields to the Argentine border.[6]

Gulf's chairman, E.D. Brockett, warned that any effort by
Bolivia to sell its nationalized oil abroad would be countered by legal
injunctions against the sale of the oil in the U.S. and other potential
markets; and he indicated also that the gas pipeline that was to have
been completed by August 1970 was "certainly up in the air."[7] Moreover, with Gulf tankers boycotting the oil pipeline terminus at Arica,
petroleum production reportedly was curtailed.

The drying up of foreign investment in Bolivia compelled the
revolutionary government to moderate its approach to Gulf. Agreements were reached between September 1970 and January 1971 on the
company's claims, providing for indemnification of about $122 million.[8]
With the opening of negotiations, Gulf tankers resumed shipping of
crude oil from Arica to the west coast of the United States.

PERU

An agreement was reached in February 1974 with the U.S. government under which Peru will make a $150 million cash payment in compensation for the properties of 11 U.S. companies that were taken over in recent years.[9] The agreement was signed by James R. Greene, special envoy of President Nixon on investment matters, who headed the U.S. negotiating team.

Of the $150 million, $74 million will be paid directly to five companies. The remaining $76 million will be paid to the U.S. government for distribution among 11 companies, including the five claimants mentioned above, for assets taken over by the military regime of Peru. The Lima government indicated that the company claims totaled about $300 million, or twice the value of the final settlement. President Nixon called the agreement a "successful outcome" to difficult negotiations. He said the dispute had "clouded relations between our two governments for the past five years." Other official U.S. government sources admitted that the agreement was "the best of a bad bargain."[10] Excluded from the settlement was International Petroleum Corporation, an Exxon subsidiary, whose properties were confiscated when the military junta seized power in 1968.

Cerro Corporation, the main enterprise affected by this agreement, estimated the book value of its affected properties at $145 million. C. Gordon Murphy, Cerro's president, said the company received $58 million from Peru and expected to receive an additional $8-10 million from the lump sum payment to be made by Peru to the U.S. government. Cerro will claim a capital loss from the settlement that it will carry forward to offset taxable income over the next 10 years. The company initiated negotiations in 1971 to sell all or part of its Peruvian subsidiary, Cerro de Pasco, on extended payment terms and offered to help manage the operation as long as requested; but Murphy announced in September 1973 that his company had broken off negotiations with the Peruvian government on the proposed sale of its mining subsidiary. The government headed by President Juan Velasco Alvarado, according to Murphy, had unilaterally established unacceptable conditions for settlement and had harassed Cerro de Pasco with measures such as sudden changes in its tax base in a "transparent effort to lower the price which Cerro would be forced to accept."[11] In August 1973, Foreign Minister Miguel de la Flor declared that Peru would pay only $12 million for the entire operation; and on 1 January 1974, Cerro de Pasco was nationalized by decree.

W.R. Grace, a diversified international company founded in Peru in 1854, claimed $26 million for two sugar plantations taken in 1969 and and listed a $31 million book value for its chemical and paper operations in the country.[12] Both Cerro and W. R. Grace have recently adopted the policy of disinvesting in Latin America and redeploying the assets in the United States.

NOTES

1. World Oil (15 August 1963): 58.

2. New York Times, 17 May 1964, p. 14.

3. Nationalization, Expropriation, and Other Takings of United States and Certain Foreign Property Since 1960, U. S. Department of State, Bureau of Intelligence and Research, (Recs-14), 30 November 1971, p. 21.

4. A good historical account of the Bolivian-foreign investor relationships is given in Wolf Radmann, "Nationalizations in Bolivia, " unpublished manuscript, spring 1972 (Department of Government, Texas Southern University).

5. Gulf Oil Co., Annual Report 1969, pp. 3-4.

6. T.D. Lumpkin, "Expropriation of Gulf Oil in Bolivia, " The Latin Americanist 6, no. 4 (June 1971): 6.

7. Wall Street Journal, 31 October 1969, p. 7.

8. Lumpkin, op. cit.

9. Wall Street Journal, 20 February 1974, p. 4.

10. Merchants National Bank, International Newsletter (March 1974).

11. Business Week, 29 September 1973, p. 31.

12. Latin American Report 2, no. 2 (September 1973): 7.

AGRARIAN REFORM LAW OF 3 JUNE 1959

Compania Ganadera Becerra (King Ranch), cattle ranch
San Andres Ranch (Summer Pingree and family), cattle ranch
St. Mark's Land Cattle Co. (Jack Everhart), cattle ranch
All sugar cane lands of companies operating mills

LAW OF NATIONALIZATION OF 6 JULY 1960

Compania Cubana de Electricidad (Cuban Electric Co., American
    Foreign Power).
Compania Cubana de Telefonos (Cuban Telephone Co., ITT).
Equipos Telefonicos Standard de Cuba, S.A. (ITT subsidiary manu-
    facturing assembler telephone components).
Sinclair Cuba Oil Co., S.A., petroleum storage facilities, distribu-
    tion system.
Esso Standard Oil, S.A. (Standard Oil of New Jersey), petroleum
    refinery, storage facilities, distribution system.
Texas Co. (West Indies) Ltd., petroleum refinery, storage facilities,
    distribution system.
Sugar companies (excludes lands nationalized by agrarian reform law):
    Atlantica del Golfo, S.A.
    Baragua Industrial Corp.
    Central Cunagua S.A. (American Sugar Refining)
    Central Ermita, S.A.
    Cia. Agricola San Sebastian (Cuban-American Sugar Co.)
    Cia. Azucarera Cespedes
    Cia. Azucarera Soledad
    Cia. Central Altagracia of West Indies
    Cia. Cubana S.A.
    Cia. Azucarera Vertientes-Camaguey
    Cuban-American Sugar Co.
    Cuban Trading Co.

U.S. Congress, House, Committee on Foreign Affairs,
Claims of U.S. Nationals Against the Government of Cuba, Hearings
before the Sub-committee on Inter-American Affairs, 88th Cong.,
2nd sess., 1964, pp. 41-44.

Florida Industrial Corp. of New York
Francisco Sugar Co.
General Sugar Estates
Guantanamo Sugar Co.
Macareno Industrial Corp. of New York
Manati Sugar Co.
Miranda Sugar Sales Co.
New Tuimucu Sugar Co.
Punta Alegre Sugar Co.
United Fruit Co.
Banks:
Chase Manhattan Bank
First National City Bank of New York
First National Bank of Boston
Burrus Flour Mills, flour milling
Reynolds International de Cuba S.A., regional office
Moore Business Forms de Cuba, business forms
West Indies Perlite Manufacturing Corp., building materials
Manufacturers General Electric S.A., electrical supplies
Union Light Power Co. of Cuba
Cia. Antilante de Lanchajes S.A.
Petrolco Cruz Verde S.A., petroleum exploration
Cia. Cubana de Minas y Minerales S.A., minerals
Bethlehem Cuba Iron Mines and Co., iron ore
Havana Coal Co., coal
Regla Coal and Co. of Cuba S.A., coal
Consolidated Development Corp., petroleum exploration
Sun Oil Co., petroleum exploration
Kewanee Inter-American Oil Co., petroleum exploration
Cuban Gulf Oil Co., petroleum exploration
Atlantic Refining Co., petroleum exploration
ATESA Drilling Co.
Exploration Incorporated Rayflex
Haliburton Oil Well Cementing Co.
John Bros. Co.
Productos Shulton de Cuba, S.A., toilet articles
Max Factor Co., cosmetics
Cuba Nickel Co., S.A., Nickel Processing Corp., U.S. government-
    owned nickel plants
Cuban Air Products Corp., oxygen equipment
Orientes Products Corp.
Servicios de Gomas Pioneer, S.A. (Pioneer Tire Co.), tire recapping
Compania Gas Liquido, S.A., liquid petroleum gas
Gas Popular de Cuba, S.A., liquid petroleum gas
H.D. Roosen Co., S.A.

Polyplasticos Industriales, S.A.
Sika Industrio-Quimica, S.A.
Home Products of Cuba, Inc.
Peison Romsi and Cia.
Armco International Corp., iron and steel products
Mohawk Iron and Steel Corp., iron and steel products
Fundacion MacFarlane, S.A. (J. MacFarlane and family) foundry
Reynolds Aluminum Co. of Cuba, aluminum foil and other products
Manufacturers Kawneer de Cuba, S.A. (Kawneer Co.), aluminum
  products
Productos de Cobre de Cuba, S.A. (Phelps-Dodge Corp.), copper wire
Ventanas de Caribe S.A., aluminum windows
National Paper and Type Co. of Cuba, S.A., paper and paper products
Compania Papelera Flamingo, S.A., paper and paper products
Cuban American Metals Distributors, Inc.
International Carbon and Ink, S.A., paper
Industrias Metalicas y Electricas S.A.
Palm Clothing Co., clothing
Cia. Nacional de Huatas, S.A.
Elliot Knitting Mills, Inc., of Cuba, S.A., textiles
Exquisite Form Brassiere of Cuba, S.A., clothing
Tejidos Nina, S.A., textiles
Fabricantes de Colchones Americanos, S.A., bedding
Cia. Onix de Cuba, S.A.
Consolidated Textile Mills, Inc., textiles
Consolidated Textile Mills, Inc., textiles
Arrocera Texita S.A., rice mills
Cia. de Refresco Canada Dry, S.A., beverages
Pan American Standard Brands, Inc., yeast
Cuba Grapefruit, Inc.
Rancho Products Corp.
Alquizar Pineapple Co., Inc., pineapple
General Distributors, S.A.
Supermercados Eklon S.A., supermarket
F.W. Woolworth Co., merchandising
Sears, Roebuck and Co., merchandising
Compania de Ferrocarril de Puerto Padre, railway
Hershey Cuban Railway Co., S.A., railway
Armour and Co., fertilizers
Cia. de Cemento Cubana Portland (Lone Star Cement Co.), cement
  producer
Cia. de Vidrio Owens-Illinois, S.A. (Owens-Illinois Glass Co.),
  glass containers
Continental Can Corp., metal containers
Cia. Goodrich de Cuba (Goodrich Rubber Co.), rubber tires

Firestone Tire and Rubber Co. of Cuba S.A., rubber tires
Cia. Embotelladoro Coca-Cola, S.A., beverages
Minimax Supermercados, S.A., supermarkets
Schering Pharmaceuticals of Cuba, pharmaceuticals
Abbott Laboratories de Cuba, pharmaceuticals
E.R. Squibb and Sons, pharmaceuticals
Cuban American Line Supply Co.
Insurance companies:
    Pan American Life Insurance Co.
    Cia. de Seguros de Ingenios, S.A.
    United States Life Insurance Co.
    American Insurance Co.
    Commercial Insurance of Newark, N.J.
    The Home Insurance Co.
    Insurance Co. of North America
    Johnson and Higgins, S.A.
    Seguros Frenkel de Cuba, S.A.
    American Insurance Underwriters of Cuba, S.A.
    Occidental Life Insurance Co.
    American National Insurance Co.
    The Employer's Fire Insurance
    Firemen's Insurance Co. of Newark
    Great American Insurance Co.
    The Hanover Fire Insurance Co.
    Hartford Fire Insurance Co.
    Maryland Casualty Co.
    National Union Fire of Pittsburgh
    Phoenix Insurance Co. of Hartford
    Queen Insurance Co., Ltd., of America
    Saint Paul Fire and Marine Insurance
    Security Insurance Co. of New Haven
    The Unity Fire and General Insurance
    United States Fire Insurance Co.
    Eagle Fire Co. of New York
    American Surety Co.
    American International Insurance Co.
    National Fire Insurance of Hartford
Machinery, motor vehicles, accessories, and parts:
    Power Machinery Co., S.A.
    Power Equipment, S.A.
    International Harvester of Cuba
    W.M. Anderson Trading Co., S.A.
    Willys Distributors, S.A.
    Agencia de Tractores y Equipos
    Iberia Machinery Co., S.A.

Autos Volkswagen de Cuba, S.A.
Piezas y Accessorios K.W., S.A.
The United Shoe Machinery Co.
Remington Rand de Cuba, S.A.
La Antillana, Cia. Comercial de Creditos, S.A.
Otis Elevator Co.
Fiberglass Distributors, Inc.
Compania de Ensamblaje de Aires Acondicionados, A.S.
Creditos y Descuentos Mercantiles, S.A. (Ford Motor Co.),
    financing company
General Motors Acceptance Corp., S.A., financing company
Colon Independent Trading Corp., financing company
Kodak Cubana, Ltd.
Railway Express Agency, Inc.
Hacienda San Andres, S.A., agriculture
American Hatchery and Farms Co., S.A., agriculture
Lone Star Farms, S.A., agriculture
Granja Los Americanos, S.A., agriculture
Lykes Bros. Inc., agriculture
Simmons International, Ltd., mattresses
Cuban Land and Leaf Tobacco, Inc., tobacco
Calixto Lopez Cia., Inc., tobacco
Rothchild-Samuel-Suignan, S.A., tobacco
Duys and Co. Havana Tobacco Co., Inc., tobacco
Rupping Havana Tobacco Co., S.A., tobacco
Standard Havana Tobacco Co., S.A., tobacco
Tabacalera Cubana, S.A., tobacco
Rey del Mundo Cigar Co., tobacco
Cia. Tabacalera de Rancho Boyeros, S.A., tobacco
Hotels, restaurants, bars:
    Hoteles Internacionales, S.A.
    Casino de Capri, S.A.
    Presidente Corp., S.A.
    Restaurant Eden Roc., S.A.
    Isle of Pines Enterprises, S.A.
    Compania de Hoteles La Riviera de Cuba, S.A.
    Intercontinental Hotels Corp. of Cuba
    Cia. Hotelera Shepard, S.A.
    Hotel Casino Deauville, S.A.
    Hoteles Hilton de Cuba, S.A.
    Hipodromo Jockey Club de Cuba, S.A.
Tintoreria Lux, S.A., dry cleaning
Lavanderia La Cubana, laundry
Tintoreria y Lavanderia Panam, S.A., dry cleaning, laundry
Caribbean Merchandising Co.

Filtrona Cubana, S.A.
Pan American Protecting Service, S.A.
Havana Docks Corp.
Standard Fruit and Steamship Co.

LAW 890 OF 14 OCTOBER 1960

Crusellas y Cia., S.A. (Colgate, Palmolive Peet), toilet articles
Cia. Mennen de Cuba, S.A., toilet articles
Envases Industriales y Comerciales S.A. (W.R. Grace and Co.),
  specialties and paper containers
Pittsburgh Plate Glass International, S.A., glass sales
Sherwin Williams Co. of Cuba, S.A., paints, varnishes
DuPont Inter-American Chemical Co., Inc., paints, varnishes
American Agricultural Chemical Co., fertilizers
Tubos de Aluminio, S.A. (Colgate, Palmolive Peet), tubes for
  toiletries
The Bohon Trading Corp.
Pan American Products
Cia. Litografica de la Habana, S.A.
Gold Seal Hosiery, hosiery
Tejidos Soltex, textiles
Ribbon Fabric Co. of Cuba, S.A.
Swift and Co., meatpacking
Los Precios Fijos, S.A.
Ferrocarriles Consolidados de Cuba, S.A. (consolidated railways
  of Cuba)
Readers Digest (printing presses leased to expropriated firm)

FIRMS INTERVENED

Cia. Antillana de Acero (10 percent U.S.-owned), manufacturing iron
  and steel rods
Cia. Concordia Textile, textiles
Cia. Industrial de Goma, rubber products
Cia. Pepsi-Cola de Cuba (Pepsi-Cola International), soft drink bottles
U.S. Rubber Co. Ltd., rubber shoes and products; tires and tubes
Moa Bay Mining Co. (Freeport Nickel-Sulphur), nickel and cobalt

OPIC (continued), 150,
153, 154; as policy instrument, 142-144
Ovando Candia, Alfredo, 158

PEMEX, 38, 58
Peterson Report, 141
Phillippi, Julio, 154
Pinochet, Ugarte, Augusto,
153
Place, John, 78, 94
political risk insurance.
See OPIC
Porfirian Era, achievements,
35-38; cientificos, 35, 36,
40; foreign investments
during, 34; Mining Code of
1884 and 1892, 49-50, 135
Pozzio, Antulio, 157

Reynolds, C.W., 92
Rogers, William P., 123
Roosevelt, Franklin D., 15,
136
Royal Dutch-Shell Group, 22,
50, 54
Rubottom, Roy, 118

Saenz, Raul, 155
Salera, Virgil, 145
Sanders, Thomas, 66
Scheer, Robert, 12
Schmitt, Karl, 140
Sigmund, Paul, 103, 126
Smith, Robert F., 118, 121
Soviet Union. See USSR
Special Copper Tribunal, 90,
114-115, 134
Standard Oil Company (N.J.),
22, 50, 52-53, 54, 124,
136, 159, 161
Suarez, Facundio, 157
Sunkel, Osvaldo, 7

Trouyet, Carlos, 46

Unidad Popular, 64, 88, 102
United States, aims in Latin
America, 139; Cuban sugar
quota, 118, 134, 136; embargo
of Cuba, 118-119, 123, 136;
evaluation of foreign investment
policies, 145-148; foreign tax
credit, 144-145; investments
in Chile, 109-111; investments
in Cuba, 15-17, 20-22, 30-31,
111-112; investments in Latin
America, 147; investments in
Mexico, 36-38, 43; "low profile" posture, 139, 141;
response to Chilean expropriations, 124-126, 136 (see also
Alliance for Progress)
Urrutia, Enrique, 115
Urrutia, Manuel, 117
USSR, 117, 118-119, 120, 121-
122, 136; Trade and Payments
Agreement with Cuba, 118

Velasco Alvarado, Juan, 160
Vera Valenzuela, Mario, 73
Vernon, Raymond, 34, 36, 149

Wallich, Henry C., 12-13
Weintraub, Sidney, 5
Wionczek, Miguel S., 7
World Bank. See IBRD
Wright, Harry K., 43

Zeitlein, Maurice, 12

ERIC N. BAKLANOFF is Board of Visitors research professor of economics at the University of Alabama. From 1950-54 he was associated with the International Division of Chase Manhattan Bank, including three years with its Puerto Rican branches. He directed Vanderbilt's Graduate Center for Latin American Studies (1962-65) and the Latin American Studies Institute (1965-68) at Louisiana State University and was a member of the economics faculty at both universities. From 1969-73, Dr. Baklanoff served as dean for international studies and programs at the University of Alabama.

His article have appeared in Economic Development and Cultural Change, National Tax Journal, Mining Engineering, Journal of Inter-American Studies, Revista Brasileira de Economia, and other professional reviews. Dr. Baklanoff edited and contributed to New Perspectives of Brazil (Nashville, Tenn.: Vanderbilt University Press, 1966) and The Shaping of Modern Brazil (Baton Rouge, La.: Louisiana State University Press, 1969).

A former president of the Southeastern Conference on Latin American Studies (1963-64), Dr. Baklanoff has been the recipient of numerous awards, including a Fulbright grant for research in Chile (1957); NDEA, Ford Foundation, and LSU Foundation grants; and a fellowship (1964-65) from the Center for Advanced Study in the Behavioral Sciences at Palo Alto. He received his Ph.D. from Ohio State University.

RELATED TITLES
Published by
Praeger Special Studies

EXPROPRIATION OF U. S. PROPERTY IN SOUTH AMERICA: Nationalization of Oil and Copper Companies in Peru, Bolivia, and Chile
George M. Ingram

THE ECONOMIC DEVELOPMENT OF REVOLUTIONARY CUBA: Strategy and Performance
Archibald R. M. Ritter

THE CHILEAN RESPONSE TO FOREIGN INVESTMENT
Stephen F. Lau

THE POLITICAL RISKS FOR MULTINATIONAL ENTERPRISE IN DEVELOPING COUNTRIES: With a Case Study of Peru
Dolph Warren Zink

THE MULTINATIONAL CORPORATION AS A FORCE IN LATIN AMERICAN POLITICS: A Case Study of the International Petroleum Company in Peru
Adalberto J. Pinelo